THE I CHING

THE I CHING

Points of Balance
and Cycles of Change

Peggy Jones

KARNAC

First published in 2008 by
Karnac Books Ltd
118 Finchley Road, London NW3 5HT

British Library Cataloguing in Publication Data

A C.I.P. for this book is available from the British Library

ISBN 978 1 85575 641 0

Edited, designed and produced by The Studio Publishing Services Ltd,
www.studiopublishingservicesuk.co.uk
e-mail: studio@publishingservicesuk.co.uk
Printed and bound in Great Britain by the MPG Books Group

www.karnacbooks.com

CONTENTS

ACKNOWLEDGEMENTS

My debt to the Richard Wilhelm edition of the *I Ching* is immeasurable and everywhere evident. I wish particularly to thank Princeton University Press for permitting me to quote from the *Shuo Kua/Discussion of the Trigrams* section in Book III. I have followed Wilhelm's names for the sixty-four hexagrams, occasionally adding an additional designation in parentheses.

I am extremely grateful to Coleman Barks for granting me permission to quote from his wonderful translation (with John Moyne), *The Essential Rumi*.

Thanks to Humanics Publishing Group for permission to use a brief quote from *The Tao of Leadership*, by John Heider.

I am also grateful to Faber and Faber, London, for granting me permission to include extracts from T. S. Eliot's *Collected Poems 1909–1962* in editions of this book sold outside the USA.

Acknowledgement has been made on the copyright page to Harcourt for permission to include the same extracts from *Collected Poems 1909–1962*, by T. S. Eliot, in editions of the book sold in the USA and its territories, and to Shambhala for permission to include extracts from *Lao Tzu, Tao Te Ching: A Book About the Way and the Power of the Way*, by Ursula K. LeGuin.

I have made many attempts to trace the copyright holders of *Desert Wisdom: Sayings from the Desert Fathers,* but to no avail. I apologize if there are avenues I should have explored. I have included the very brief extract in spite of this omission.

The same is true of the lines attributed to Mencius with which the Introduction begins. These lines appear in *Looking for the Golden Needle: An Allegorical Journey,* by Gerda Geddes.

Friends, colleagues, and family have been unfailingly supportive and interested in the progress of the book, and I want them to know that I was more appreciative than they can imagine and than I perhaps managed to express at the time. Above all, I wish to thank my husband, Hugh, for his enduring belief in me and in this book. His encouragement and assistance has been unstinting and unqualified and I could not have done it without him.

ABOUT THE AUTHOR

Born in Philadelphia, Pennsylvania, Peggy Jones moved to London in 1965. She trained first at the Westminster Pastoral Foundation and subsequently with the Society of Analytical Psychology. Having worked with the Richard Wilhelm *I Ching* for twenty-five years, and following her retirement from analytic practice, she took the first steps towards writing this version of the Book of Changes. She lives in Richmond, Surrey.

Introduction

If you know the point of balance,
You can settle the details.
If you can settle the details,
You can stop running around.
If you can stop running around,
Your mind will become calm.
If your mind becomes calm,
You can think in front of the tiger.
If you can think in front of the tiger,
You will surely succeed.

attributed to Mencius, contemporary of
Confucius (Geddes, 1995)

The point of balance is a living, moving centre, which is as real as it is indefinable. Yet we know it when we feel it, when we find it, and, like dominoes falling in a single, multiple shift, the details become ordered and clear; we experience a sense of quiet 'knowing', the mind sheds its confusion and we can face whatever we fear, whatever challenges or threatens us. We have 'succeeded', regardless of the outcome of events, because we have found, in

T. S. Eliot's memorable phrase, 'the still point of the turning world', the place where the 'dance' is, Here and Now (Eliot, 1963). At its most extreme, this dynamic balance may expose us to conflict and confusion, which threatens to overwhelm us, as we feel ourselves to be torn apart by events, inner or outer. At its most blessed, we may find the subtlety and delicacy and beauty and appropriateness of life and death to be almost unbearably 'perfect'. In between is where our daily experiences require us to make choices and to live with those choices in an ordinary but responsible way, and the greater our self-awareness is, the more highly developed our sensitivity to others and to all the balances of the world, the more enlightened and meaningful will be our choices.

The world offers us little guidance, however, in this matter of choosing between different paths. On the contrary, it plays on our fears, seeks to shape our desires, and presses us forward into a powerfully imagined but non-existent future. Many, if not most of us, at one time or another experience dissatisfaction with our lives, with the misfit between an inner sense of self – of some possibility or promise of meaning or fulfilment – and the outer realizations of life, the relative superficiality of our choices, the lack of care and compassion that is manifested in most human relationships and in our contact with the non-human world. There are few places to turn if we are seeking examples of other ways of moving through life, less fearful, more gentle, more informed, more joyous ways.

One of the 'places' where many have sought wisdom or clarification over the millennia is in the pages of the *I Ching*. Emerging from the distant, unrecorded past into the world of dates and names about 3000 years ago in China, the *I Ching* is a book of wisdom, a body of commentaries to which many individuals have contributed over the centuries. The *I Ching* is also – and less well – known as the Book of Changes, and this latter title reflects its vision and nature much better than the former, which, in its English translation at least, emphasizes the impression of thing-ness and permanence, which is at once so longed-for and so misleading. In spite of recognizing that Life arises out of, and is nourished by, the dynamic interplay of the opposites, creating the innumerable forms and conditions of Life and also its problems and suffering, we tend to seek a more static balance; we try to 'fix' things and hope they will stay fixed, frequently creating more problems than we solve by so doing.

In fact, at all times and in all places, the only certain statement we can make about life is that it is an unending process of things coming together and then coming apart, birth and death, growth and decay, expansion and contraction: impermanence is the nature of conditioned existence. How do we achieve the dynamic balance that is required by life if we are not to succumb to helplessness and depression, on the one hand, in the face of a changing world and the certainty of our personal death, or to feverish, exhausting, and ultimately futile attempts to avoid or outrun those realities on the other?

The answer must lie in the act of choosing, in the belief that the choices we make – consciously, in the present, without blinding ourselves to what 'is' – are significant. We shape the landscapes of our own and other lives to a greater extent than we are, perhaps, comfortable acknowledging, and thus bear collective responsibility for the balances that we allow to inform our journey through life, the manner in which we make ourselves available for Life to live through us. No choice is insignificant, no life more or less important than another. When we throw the coins or divide the yarrow stalks we gather all the strands of movement and energy in which we are participating into a momentary pause, a point of potential balance, and by so doing we are effectively stating our desire and intention to become more aware, to act more carefully and with more attention to how our choices will affect and reflect our lives and goals.

Consulting the I Ching

No matter how much our thoughts and fantasies may be drawn to the future, with dread or anticipation, or to the past, with regret or nostalgia, we can only live in the present; choices can only be made now. When we consult the I Ching we are bringing ourselves quietly to a focused point of attention in the present and seeking to learn or to be shown how to understand and move forward from this point in the most enlightened way. Through this process we may glimpse the route by which we arrived at this moment, and we might also gain a sense of the direction in which our choices could lead, but the focus must remain steadfastly on now.

For this reason, the time we spend in preparing ourselves to throw the coins is vitally important. We are choosing to place ourselves consciously, carefully, and thoughtfully at the centre of this moment. We gather ourselves and our thoughts, review the situation in which we find ourselves and what effect it seems to be having, reflect on the nature of the particular worry or question that has been the immediate cause for turning to the *Book of Changes*, and then we throw the coins. This profound focusing and quietening of the mind and body creates an atmosphere of sincerity and readiness, of openness and honesty which is of great benefit in itself and in the establishment of a meaningful connection to oneself, to the wisdom of the book and to the wisdom within.[1]

Once this process of gathering seems completed, it is useful to just let it go, breathe deeply but quietly for a moment, and then throw the coins. The mechanics of a throw are as follows (for instruction in the use of yarrow stalks see Appendix C).

Three coins of the same denomination are used. Pennies are appropriate as they are a fundamental unit of currency. One side of the coin will represent Heaven and the other side Earth. The Heaven side is given the numerical value three, and the Earth side is given the value two. (It does not matter which sides are chosen to represent Heaven or Earth, as long as we are consistent in the attribution. As Heaven is considered to represent a more 'masculine' energy – yang – and Earth a more 'feminine' – yin – energy, it follows that if a portrait appears on one side, then the gender of that image might provide the rationale for choosing in a particular way.)

The coins are thrown six times to construct a hexagram. The first throw will be represented by the bottom line, and the five further throws will become the lines above it. In this way the hexagram grows from the bottom up, as does a tree. The numerical value of each line should be noted and a solid or broken line should be written beside the number, depending on whether the total is an even number (broken line) or an odd number (solid line). In that the values of either side of the coin are two or three, in any given throw one of the following combinations will be obtained:

$$2+2+2 = 6$$
$$2+2+3 = 7$$
$$2+3+3 = 8$$
$$3+3+3 = 9$$

For example, let us consider the case where the six throws have yielded, from the bottom up, 9, 7, 7, 8, 9, 6. The resulting hexagram would have a solid line in the first three places, then a broken one, then a solid one, and, finally, a broken one at the top. It would look like this:

all tails 6th throw   6   ▬▬ ▬▬   →
5th throw   9   ▬▬▬▬▬   →
4th throw   8   ▬▬ ▬▬
3rd throw   7   ▬▬▬▬▬
2nd throw   7   ▬▬▬▬▬
all heads 1st throw   9   ▬▬▬▬▬   →

The lines that result from throws having all heads or all tails – or, to give them their numerical values, nine and six – are considered to be Moving or Changing Lines. As the forms of the present moment are continually dissolving and evolving into the forms of the next moment, the Changing Lines represent the edge of that alteration, the place where the form is collapsing, where it has gone as far as it can go in one direction, developed to its limit. In the terms of the *I Ching*, at this point yang becomes yin and vice versa. For example, a yang line, constructed of three threes, could not become more yang and would have to become yin. In fact, a nine is known as an 'old yang' line and a six is known as an 'old yin' line. When they change, they will become 'young yin', in the first instance, and 'young yang' in the second. (Seven and eight are both considered to be 'young' and are not Changing Lines; they reflect a fairly stable situation in which further development is possible before any major change of emphasis is likely to occur.) When these lines are taken into consideration, a second hexagram – the *evolved* hexagram – will be constructed, having a broken line at the bottom, then two solid lines and a broken one, as before. In the fifth position, the original solid line will have become a broken one and, at the top, the original broken line is now solid. This new 'picture' may be seen as another way of looking at the original, or as a possible development of it, or as a sort of 'pointer', indicating the place where the 'action' is, or where the point of balance has been disturbed or is changing. Side by side, the original and the evolved hexagrams would look like this:

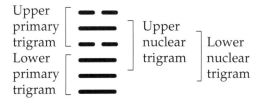

Original   *Evolved*

In order to consult the *I Ching*, we look at the hexagram both in its entirety and, particularly initially, as a combination of two primary trigrams, the lower one and the upper. (There are two nuclear trigrams that may be considered as well. They overlap within the hexagram and are comprised of the second, third and fourth lines, in the case of the lower nuclear trigram, and the third, fourth and fifth lines, in the case of the upper nuclear trigram.)

Upper primary trigram / Upper nuclear trigram / Lower primary trigram / Lower nuclear trigram

Turning to the Grid (see Appendix E), we locate the point of intersection of the two primary trigrams. In the case we are considering, the lower trigram is *Ch'ien* and the upper one is *K'an*, and they intersect at the number five. This is the number of the hexagram thrown, and we turn to the pages that comment on this hexagram to read the text. When we get to the part called The Changing Lines, we read only those that refer to this particular hexagram, that is 9/1st, 9/5th, and 6/top. Following this, we consult the Grid again with reference to the second/*evolved* hexagram (see above). The lower trigram is now *Sun* and the upper is *Kên*; they intersect at the number eighteen. Turning to the appropriate page, we read only the text, as there are no longer any Changing Lines.

5. *Hsü*/Waiting   18. *Ku*/Work on what has been spoiled

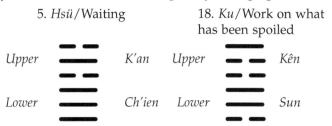

To repeat, as the coins are thrown and totalled, both the numerical value of the throw and its linear representation should be noted, always starting at the bottom. In this way confusion is avoided around the changing lines. Small arrows may be placed alongside the nine or the six, pointing to the right to indicate that this line is changing, causing the hexagram to develop into the *evolved* hexagram.

Movement within the hexagram can be seen to be the result of a number of separate processes: first, there is the movement from bottom to top. Lines are considered to enter at the bottom, in the first position, to move upwards through the positions or places, and to exit from the top, the sixth position. Thus, the urge to grow and move, so characteristic of life, is taken as a given within the situation of each hexagram. This movement will be conditioned, however, by the natural tendencies and characteristics of each line. (See Appendix B for explanation.) Second, there is movement associated with each trigram, ascending or descending or stationary, and this will be considered in the text. This aspect of movement may result in the trigrams intensifying or counteracting the natural inclination of each. Finally, there is the movement that will be associated with the hexagram as a whole, which will be a reflection of the particular times pictured. This final aspect of movement is, therefore, the most important, and it may overshadow all other considerations based on position or natural attributes.

Interpreting the Throw

As explored in greater detail below, the meaning that we find in a particular throw of the coins – the meaning we 'make' of a throw – will always be the result of a creative encounter between the individual and the imagery of any particular hexagram. As every individual is different, so every hexagram and its constituent trigrams will carry a penumbra of 'meanings'. Rarely will all comments seem equally accurate, congruent, or significant. The most helpful attitude to bring to the *I Ching* is one of openness, curiosity, and a willingness to consider new ideas.

The commentary on each hexagram will cover some or all of the following areas.

1. Images or specific dynamics associated with this hexagram. These characteristics are similar to the first impressions we might have of a dream upon waking – its 'tone' or the impression it leaves – before the details are recalled.
2. Calendar or seasonal associations to the hexagram that may contribute to the overall 'feel' of the situation represented. These associations should be noted lightly but not allowed to dominate the sense of meaning that may emerge from a reading.
3. Attributes of the primary (or nuclear) trigrams that may shape our understanding of the situation. Reference is made in a number of places to the Inner World Arrangement of the trigrams, which appears in the *Shuo Kua/Discussion of the Trigrams*. This section of Wilhelm's edition contains an ancient saying that reflects a dynamic interpretation of the flow of creative energy (or 'God') represented through the eight foundation trigrams, *Ch'ien*, the Creative, *K'un*, the Receptive, *Chên*, the Arousing, *K'an*, the Abysmal, *Kên*, Keeping Still, *Sun*, the Gentle, *Li*, the Clinging, *Tui*, the Joyous. (For further discussion of the Inner World Arrangement, see Appendix A.) The saying is as follows:

> God comes forth in the sign of the Arousing; he brings all things to completion in the sign of the Gentle; he causes creatures to perceive one another in the sign of the Clinging (light); he causes them to serve one another in the sign of the Receptive. He gives them joy in the sign of the Joyous; he battles in the sign of the Creative; he toils in the sign of the Abysmal; he brings them to perfection in the sign of Keeping Still.'

4. Reflections on all of this material, its energy, the 'story' it is telling, and how we might recognize or think about that which is being presented symbolically within our own ordinary, real lives.

Having read the general commentary, we turn to the Changing Lines, if it is appropriate; that is, if we have thrown a six or a nine. These lines have an extra dynamic to them; they reflect areas where shifts are happening more rapidly or more dramatically, or where we need to be more specifically attentive. They may suggest a direction or a nuance of the situation that we might have otherwise overlooked. It is important to spend a little time with these brief paragraphs before moving on to read the commentary of the evolved hexagram, the second hexagram, which is a development of aspects of the first or original hexagram.

The meaningful interpretation of any hexagram depends ultimately on the development of a capacity for inner reflection and conversation: that is, the establishment and evolution of self-engagement and self-knowledge. At all times, the individual must seek to be open and honest with herself about herself; she must exercise curiosity and learn to follow her imagination wherever it leads, while holding on to the Ariadne-thread of self-awareness. This suggests a sort of oscillation between hearing the 'prompt' in the written word on the page (or sensing an inner resonance to a particular image) and moving within to learn more about that connection. This back-and-forth movement will soon become instinctive, so that we no longer seek the meaning outside ourselves, nor do we construct it within; we find meaning and we create it, and the process is allowed to move as it will, appearing and disappearing, developing further or, apparently, slipping away.

In spite of the fact that the process of consulting the *I Ching* is such a personal and self-contained exercise, some people find they are afraid of the outcome of a reading, afraid the *I Ching* will tell them something they do not want to hear, or instruct them to do something they do not want to do. This fear is held consciously and is, therefore, accessible for consideration and reflection before the coins are thrown. We all need to entertain doubts about even our most cherished or well-developed plans or projects. When we exclude doubt we force ourselves to wear blinkers, like a highly-strung horse that might take fright and bolt. We unintentionally create heavy baggage when we do this, as we must haul our unwanted doubts around with us while they accumulate more and more power for being unexamined. They take on a life of their own the more we disown them, and we finish by dreading that everybody/anybody/the *I Ching* will confront us with these doubts, only now they will have taken on the stature of 'facts' and become reasons for not continuing on our chosen path.

The way forward is clear: name and include any and all doubts in the process of reflection, not denying them but also not giving them any particular weight. Doubts provide information about how we view ourselves and the world; they are internal and personal, and the 'charge' they carry varies widely between individuals. When we can allow our doubts to exist, not attempting to talk ourselves out of them but also not permitting them to close down or sidetrack our development, when we can look at what we are afraid of in a compassionate but neutral way, it begins to loosen its grip on us and we see it for what it is, a fear, not a fact.

There are times when we have prepared ourselves thoroughly for a throw, acknowledging our fears, questions, or desires, centring and reflecting on what *is* at this moment, and yet the coins give us a hexagram that seems to make no sense at all. If we feel resistant to the imagery or words, that gives us information about where we might enquire further, but if there is no resonance we are likely to feel frustrated and – understandably – dismissive of the whole process. It is important not to allow this disappointment to spoil the consultation. As always, we should acknowledge our feelings fully, giving them all the space they need without drawing any conclusions. Then we should reread the relevant paragraphs carefully, this time including the entries for the Changing Lines, even though they might not be strictly applicable according to the throw. Without any attempt to force or find meaning we should simply allow space for the reading within, and then let it go. Close the book quietly and walk away.

Note

1. It may be helpful to visualize a stage and to take time to name and place on it, or in the wings, the various concerns or individuals or situations that come to mind as we review our lives. In this way, central concerns can be placed 'centre-stage', while more peripheral issues are allotted positions appropriate to their perceived importance. The stage acts as a container for all the many aspects of a life and also provides unoccupied space. In addition, this arrangement allows for the presentation to the *I Ching* of the whole of an individual's present experience, rather than an isolated 'question' that may seem pressing but that is taken out of context and brought to the consultation without reflection.

The Tao that can be named is not the true Tao

The Hexagrams

1. Ch'ien / The Creative, Heaven

Primary Trigrams

above *Ch'ien* / The Creative, Heaven
below *Ch'ien* / The Creative, Heaven

Nuclear Trigrams

above *Ch'ien* / The Creative, Heaven
below *Ch'ien* / The Creative, Heaven

In human life, the Creative works to activate, to engender, to inspire. It raises our energy level and expands and extends our capacities. This energy is bright and sharp, often impatient with the requirements or details of a process. In fact, when we or the atmosphere around us are charged with this pure, yang energy, there may be a sense almost of invulnerability, even God-likeness. For this reason, there may well be a considerable degree of resistance to the limits imposed by human life and the conditions of the world. The process of transformation may have its roots in the Creative, but unless our awareness also undergoes an expansion the net result of such a time could be no more than the after-glow of a beautiful fireworks display.

The construction of the hexagram consists of the trigram *Ch'ien* repeated in both upper and lower positions. Both nuclear trigrams are also *Ch'ien*. This construction represents the timeless, undivided, unconditioned force of creativity. As such, it is not any thing, and is unable to become some thing without being received, modified, and given form. At that point time enters the picture as the medium, the dimension through which creativity and transformation occur. The Creative is continuous; it does not have a resting state. It is a dynamic constant, the energy of which finds expression in the innumerable finite forms that have arisen since the universe came into being. Thus, it permeates, activates, and is identical with every living thing, every process, every experience. The Creative, seamlessly and dynamically embracing and embraced by the Receptive (see *K'un*, below), each carrying the seed of the other within, constitutes Life, eternal and unopposed.

As noted above, this hexagram is constructed of six yang lines. While no balance exists in this structure, the powerful dynamic at its heart constitutes the process of life seeking manifestation. We cannot know what came before, or what will follow, whether 'constructive' or 'destructive'. Our part in the overall picture is also an unknown. None the less, when we are gripped by the need to express our creativity – to allow the Creative to express itself through us – it is unlikely to be either easy or comfortable. Whatever the area to which we feel drawn, compromise is not an option and will never satisfy us. We express our humanity and our individuality most fully in the creative act and the lack of a connection to, or channel for, our creativity can be deeply distressing.

Ch'ien is a calendar hexagram representing the fourth month of the Chinese year, May–June. In the northern hemisphere the sun is at its height and the daylight hours are at their maximum. The calendar hexagram that follows *Ch'ien* is 44, *Kou / Coming To Meet*, where a yielding line re-enters at the bottom of the hexagram indicating the beginning of the darkening of the light as the year's cycle turns towards autumn.

The Changing Lines

Dragons are associated with the trigram *Ch'ien*, and the six places of the hexagram are seen as the six dragons, or steps, that lead to wisdom and the fulfilment of the Tao. Dragons are fabulous and dangerous, wonderful, fascinating, potentially arrogant, and charismatic. They represent the untamed condition of raw energy. The changing lines picture the taming of the dragon in that they reflect the process of transformation from yang to yin. The interaction of the Receptive (see the next hexagram, *K'un*) and the Creative creates a powerful dynamic; consequently, each of the changing lines represents an exceptional time.

9/1st   In order for the tremendous potential of the Creative to be realized, it must be channelled through a form, an individual, a life. We could almost say it must open itself to doubt about its own perfection or purity; it must open to the Other. It is when we are most self-assured and confident of our direction and our goals that we are most vulnerable to the entry of radical challenge from the least expected direction – and most in need of it.

9/2nd   Too much agreement or homogeneity leaves no space for the creativity that derives from variety and challenge. Where a lively dialectic exists, there is the possibility of wholly new ideas emerging. We must be prepared to welcome dissent, passion, argument, and frustration if we wish for new visions to arise and inspire or teach us.

9/3rd   At the growing edge of our lives there is so much to learn and we have so little experience that we may find ourselves faced with the choice between dissembling, which can require a lot of energy to sustain, and simply throwing ourselves into the moment, admitting our ignorance and accepting guidance when it is genuinely offered. The lack of pretension and freshness of this path, as long as it is not contrived or calculated to elicit a particular response, is unlikely to meet with rejection or rebuff. This is not a counsel for lack of consideration of others; rather, it is for the release of any attachment we might have to our self-image or self-importance.

9/4th   In the context of this hexagram, the fourth position represents an opportunity for a conscious re-balancing of our priorities. There are times in life when we have little freedom of choice, particularly when we are children; but we rarely imagine or recognize how open the world is to us and how much effect we can have if we are prepared to work hard. The clue is to start now, with quiet determination, to take the first small step and then the next and the next, trusting that the strength to carry on will be there when we need it.

9/5th   The image associated with this line is that of a dragon flying in the sky. For the Chinese, the dragon represented all things charged with mystery and extraordinary potency. The dragon was one of the four magic animals capable of transformation and was associated with great good fortune. Its abode was the heavens. If we attempt to translate this into human terms it is bound to be difficult, as it reaches beyond all ordinary boundaries and definitions. It suggests a wild and glorious capacity for life, freed from the burden of fear, and limitless in its joy. How we apply this to ourselves is for each of us to discover.

9/top   While this firm line at the highest point of the hexagram of Heaven has been associated with arrogance, a more thoughtful reading might consider the significance of finding oneself as far from the dark of earth as it is possible to be. There is no further one can go in this direction, the only way forward is down into just the area where our deepest fears reside, the realm of the physical, of earth, of ordinary collective existence. If a person does not know how to let go and be re-absorbed, but insists on always pressing forward, there will be a hard lesson to learn. All things turn into their opposite in time; that is how time and transformation work, and learning this lesson is a first step towards wisdom.

When all the lines are nines: the hexagram will then change into *K'un*, Earth, The Receptive. By its very nature *Ch'ien* is a guiding and moving force, but is not itself visible or manifest; its effect is made visible, made manifest through the birth of all forms and creatures out of its union with *K'un*, Earth, The Receptive.

2. K'un / The Receptive, Earth

Primary Trigrams

above *K'un* / The Receptive, Earth
below *K'un* / The Receptive, Earth

Nuclear Trigrams

above *K'un* / The Receptive, Earth
below *K'un* / The Receptive, Earth

K'un is a calendar hexagram representing the ninth month, November–December. In the northern hemisphere it is the season of the year when the days are shortest and growth appears to have ceased. All is quiet. All four trigrams that constitute the hexagram are *K'un*. There are no light, yang lines. This is the opposite of the month represented by *Ch'ien*, May–June, where there are no dark, yin lines remaining in the hexagram. (See Hexagram 1, *Ch'ien* / The Creative, above.)

The relationship of the Receptive to the Creative is best illustrated not by words, but by the Taoist symbol, t'ai chi (Wilhelm, 1989, p. lv), which represents the complementarity of the two within an overall unity: a circle encloses two interlocking embryonic forms, one black, the other white. Within the black lies a white 'eye' and within the white lies a black 'eye'. The Creative and the Receptive, Yang and Yin, interpenetrate each other and are indivisible. Therefore, if we wish to discuss them we should always strive to remember that the separation is artificial, a necessary dualistic trick to enable us to explore the two energies.

If *Ch'ien* is Life as infinite creative energy, *K'un* is Life as limitless capacity, boundless receptivity. As the vessel, albeit a limitless one, *K'un* forms a bridge to the temporal. Everything we can sense or measure, think or touch, space, and the relationships between, and juxtaposition of, objects, animals, people, events, all of this is shaped within the vessel of the Receptive. However, it is the inter-penetration of *Ch'ien* and *K'un* that gives rise to these forms. The hexagrams, with their undifferentiated and homogenous structure, must effect an exchange for the six foundation trigrams, the repre-sentatives of all possible forms, to come into being and, from them, the sixty-two hexagrams that follow.

This hexagram represents a particular energy (which is more like a field or a principle) in its pure state, a state that does not exist in nature, as emphasized above. It cannot exist in human beings either, because human life is conditioned and conditioned life is shaped by the opposites. However, with these provisos in mind, we can consider how the time and conditions reflected in the hexagram might affect our lives. The season represented is late autumn, early winter, a time when the processes of the earth, which is represented by *K'un*, continue out of sight. When such a time occurs in our lives we must learn to trust the health of the 'seeds' that have been planted within us, to be patient with gradual growth and develop-ment, to be content, for the time being, with nurturing ourselves and the world in a very grounded way, using our intuition and feel-ings to perceive where our efforts are best directed, not wearing ourselves out with trying to make something happen.

On the other hand, the lack of differentiation in the hexagram may point to a lack of balance, excessive passivity or an absence of complementarity. Life cannot begin, leave alone thrive, without intercourse and, if we are over-identified with the Receptive posi-tion, we may resist the focusing and choosing that is necessary if we are to advance on our particular, individual path.

The Changing Lines

In the context of a time of rest and receptivity, the changing lines introduce an altogether different energy, representing or reminding us of the dynamic process of transformation. In each position, the penetration of a yang line and yang energy into the situation pictured in the hexagram creates an opportunity for greater consciousness and awareness of self and cosmos.

6/1st   Initial conditions, the beginnings of things, are critical to how events proceed and their outcome. The times require receptivity and complete openness, and the more we can put to one side our ideas about how things should be or what we want from the future, the more ripe will we be to receive fresh ideas or to recognize new possibilities. We forget so quickly that every moment is a 'first-time' moment that has never existed before; the seeds we plant today have never been planted before. If we did remember, we would act and choose with more care and more joy. But every moment also offers us a new opportunity to wake up. In the words of Rumi (Barks & Moyne, 1995):

> The breeze at dawn has secrets to tell you.
> Don't go back to sleep.

6/2nd All things natural fulfil themselves by becoming what they are. This may seem obvious, but if we reflect upon it further it leads us deeper and deeper into the question of what we truly are. The Zen *koan* – What is your original face? – leads to the same area of paradox and mystery. When we talk about our personal 'flow' or 'journey' we are in the same area. How do we know what it is? How do we find it? How do we become, each of us, that which we are?

6/3rd The human mind is remarkable; we have no idea how much it is capable of as we only use a fraction of it. The uses we do make of it are potentially more within our control than we are generally aware. Calming the mind, focusing it, expanding its field of awareness, disciplining it, exercising it: we can all learn ways of owning and managing the movements of our minds and increasing our consciousness if we apply ourselves.

6/4th This yielding line in a yielding position signifies a time when the energies of Earth are most deeply at rest and impenetrable, a time of contraction and darkness appropriate to the moment. Under these circumstances, if we feel suddenly moved to strong action, we should consider our motives and goals. The attraction of activity and focus is great when there is not much going on; sustained commitment to a particular course requires more than just temporary enthusiasm.

6/5th   The fifth position holds a particular prominence in the hexa-grams, often representing the ideal response to a given set of conditions. In this case, yielding and remaining open is exemplary; however, nothing remains the same for long and when a different – firmer, more clearly defined or determined – course of thought or action is indicated it will be important to recognize how far-reaching the effects of our choice might be. We should not allow ourselves to choose in a superficial or reckless way.

6/top   Change is inevitable; how we respond to it is infinitely vari-able. No matter how many times we go through the cycle of beginnings, middles, and ends in life, we will still find ourselves balking at change when it pushes us into the unknown or forces us to accept that which feels unaccept-able. Each of us represents a small but unique part of the whole of creation at every moment. The significance of our choices may be unfathomable, but it is not inconsequential.

3. Chun / Difficulty at the Beginning

Primary Trigrams

above *K'an* / The Abysmal, Water
below *Chên* / The Arousing, Thunder

Nuclear Trigrams

above *Kên* / Keeping Still, Mountain
below *K'un* / The Receptive, Earth

There is a Maori creation myth that pictures the first coupling of Heaven and Earth producing offspring who must force the cosmic parents apart in order to emerge, thereby creating the space in which life itself can exist. The story reflects the fact that birth always requires a struggle and a separation from what was before. While the process is chaotic, it is not reversible, and it carries within itself the energy to see it through, as well as the trials that make it hazardous. At first it might feel as if the new thing is almost life-threatening in its determination to undermine a previously established balance, and we may resist its efforts to pry us open and emerge, but without the drive towards visibility with which new ideas or parts of ourselves are imbued, our 'offspring' would never see the light of day.

Structurally, the image suggested by the trigrams that constitute this hexagram is of a blade of grass pushing up out of the ground. *Chên*, the Arousing, is associated with wood, and here this extends to the first shoots of grass as they emerge from the earth, represented by the three broken lines of *K'un*. This hexagram represents the first intercourse of Heaven and Earth (*Ch'ien* and *K'un*), giving rise to the eldest son, *Chên*. The obstacle that gives the hexagram its theme is the firm line in the strong fifth position. As the natural movement of *Chên* is to rise and that of both *K'an* and *K'un* is to sink, this hexagram suggests not only considerable turmoil, but also that these testing times are balanced by the assistance of naturally occurring energies.

In the very early stages of growth, when new energies or ideas are seeking expression, their nature and goals are still unknown and unformed. This may be a difficult and demanding time, but we must not try to rush things to birth before the time of gestation is completed. The time requires an act of faith in the process within which we are being transformed and held; this is also the best way to endure the uncertainty of the moment.

Finally, *K'un* represents humanity, and it is important to recognize this stage as one with which we are all familiar. This familiarity means we can help and encourage each other to persevere. When new things are being brought to birth we may well need helpers, and should not feel that our efforts are compromised by enlisting support. There is no particular virtue in 'going it alone'; the heroic attitude can make it difficult to learn from others or through the experience itself.

The Changing Lines

9/1st   Confronted with difficulty from the outset, it is sensible to seek others of like mind. This is not always easy; as we look around we may feel there are few who appear to be on the same path, few that belong to our 'tribe', and this recognition can be disheartening. We need to develop great awareness of and sensitivity towards that which draws us and we may need to do this for some time, monitoring how we respond to this idea rather than that idea, this person rather than that person, and learning about ourselves as we do so. This is a practice in itself, and it develops patience, self-discipline, and discernment.

6/2nd We may well feel overwhelmed at times by the magnitude of the task that lies before us. We doubt our ability to manage. Under these circumstances we must find a way to differentiate and limit our goals or plans, identifying manageable steps and – most importantly – stopping when we have completed them. When we lose touch with our abilities and resources we feel childlike and helpless, and our first task is to remind ourselves that we are capable of choice and action.

6/3rd   There may be a long way to go, but there are stages in any journey and if they do not occur naturally, affording us an opportunity to pause and integrate our experience so far, then it is advisable for us to take the time ourselves. The conclusion of a particular chapter is not the same as the conclusion of the book, although sometimes we resist the former because it feels like the latter. While we might say, 'If I stop I will never start again', the truth is that we cannot sustain an effort indefinitely without regular reflection and refreshment.

6/4th   There are those of us whose instinctive response to difficult times is to adapt and to look for others to lead the way. There is nothing wrong with this strategy; indeed, if we adapt willingly and follow others wholeheartedly we can contribute a great deal to any joint endeavour. However, it could become a strategy for avoiding responsibility and might, over time, lead to the loss of a sense of self. Our task is to learn while we gather confidence through following and watching others; then one day we may feel ready to take the difficult decisions ourselves and will have gathered enough knowledge and wisdom to sustain us through our own trials. In the end, nobody can do our growing for us.

9/5th   In the context of this hexagram, this line represents the danger, the challenge, but also the point of encounter with our own deepest flow and energy. When we set out on the path of growth and self-realization we are naturally setting out for a rendezvous with ourselves, and it will occur over and over again, at deeper and deeper levels. We can view ourselves as the problem or as the solution. Every time we choose the latter we open ourselves to new understandings, new growth. Choosing the former leads only to further struggle and self-criticism.

6/top   We need something to push against if we are to grow; without some resistance we don't develop the necessary musculature. But there are times in all our lives when we feel lost, aimless, at sea, with no signposts outside of us and no pressing urges inside. This is a time to experiment, to see what works for right now. We should take it moment by moment, or day by day, not placing great emphasis on 'getting it right' but simply on developing our curiosity and inventiveness and then on learning. What we discover does not have to lead on to 'greater' things; it is from the noticing of smaller things that we are likely to derive pleasure and regain an appetite for life.

4. Mêng / Youthful Folly

Primary Trigrams

above *Kên* / Keeping Still, Mountain
below *K'an* / The Abysmal, Water

Nuclear Trigrams

above *K'un* / The Receptive, Earth
below *Chên* / The Arousing, Thunder

The journey begins; it cannot fail to begin. Like a stream drawn inexorably to the sea by the force of gravity and the pull of the moon, the seeker may move in a clumsy, bumbling way initially, giving the appearance of confusion or lack of direction, yet the attraction of the Path is irresistible and, once embarked upon, will gather strength and purpose. Here *K'an*, as deep flowing water, represents both the seeker and the seeking. Before him lies the Mountain, representing the distant, unknown goal of all journeys: wisdom, self-knowledge, stillness; or, more simply, more immediately, adventure, challenge, Life itself. This is the beginning of a journey, or perhaps the renewal of a journey, and he must set forth unhesitatingly or risk turning his back on his own destiny.

The Fool is undisturbed by fears, desires, or preconceptions, and in this he resembles the Sage. Indeed, the Holy Fool, or Wise Fool, is a figure recognized at all times and in all places. In this hexagram there is an implied relationship between the Fool, or the innocent, whose journey is starting, and the Sage, or teacher, whose completed and perfected journey is symbolized by the mountain. In seeking a teacher, we demonstrate a realistic modesty, an interest in learning, and our preparedness for commitment to both the relationship and the journey. There is a saying, 'When the pupil is ready the teacher appears'. The particular quality of this relationship, with its emphasis on mutuality and interdependence, is reflected in these words.

This hexagram addresses questions and issues that arise at the start of all the innumerable renewals in the journey of Life. Its counsel – to respond to the call, to be as a 'fool', empty and therefore open, to ask for help wisely and to trust that when guidance is needed it will be provided – applies to any situation in which we need to let go of the safe and familiar and take to the road.

The Changing Lines

The Changing Lines address the relationship and appropriate behaviour between the teacher and the pupil, the Sage and the Fool. The coming-into-relationship of these two 'Beings', or ways-of-being-conscious, indicates that a journey and a dialogue has begun. Without such a dialogue – inner or outer, with oneself or with an Other – we are simply trapped in our own view, or imaginings, and our progress will be all but halted until we become opened to other possibilities.

6/1st   Long ago it was customary to make a sacrifice before setting off on a long or dangerous expedition, and the spirit of that ritual can be helpful, demonstrating, as it does, simplicity, trust, and the acknowledgement of how little we know. Pride can obscure vision and prevent learning.

9/2nd   We can nurture a sense of self-possession by being undemanding, having low expectations and rarely risking misadventure, but this will not take us far along the path towards wisdom and self-knowledge. Learning how to access and trust the language and movement of our own inner 'flow' takes time and requires us to become more visible, to take risks, to gain experience through getting it 'wrong'. It demands nothing less than wholehearted commitment.

6/3rd   We may find that our very determination to move ahead in our journey becomes a limitation if it means that we forge on without proper attention to the details of closure on previous issues or relationships. The way forward becomes confused with escape from the past, and we lose our sense of direction altogether. This may be a time to turn to others whose judgement is trustworthy and who might help us to gently reflect on our position.

6/4th In the context of this particular hexagram, the fourth position represents a time well into the journey when we lose our orientation; perhaps we lose concentration, or our sense of where we are headed, or what it was that we hoped to achieve. There may be no apparent 'shape' emerging at all, nothing to relate our efforts to. This is a testing time that requires us to reaffirm our commitment to the process of growth and learning while also surrendering to the discomfort or even distress that is our present experience.

6/5th We never know so much that what remains to be learned is not infinitely the greater sum. 'Old men ought to be explorers', wrote T. S. Eliot in 'East Coker' (Eliot, 1963). If we approach each day with curiosity and wonder, ready to be amazed and to embrace whatever comes our way, we continue to be available for life to live and create through us. If we close our eyes or minds or hearts, we may lose the capacity for delight and surprise and may find ourselves becoming hard, even disillusioned. This can be a lonely position, at any age.

9/top We readily appreciate the potential that lies in children, yet seem to consider that at a certain point – when we are 'adults' – it is no longer appropriate to have dreams, to be prepared to start afresh; it is almost as if we do not believe that the potential exists any more. The difference may be that we must search more deeply for what feels to be a true direction, work harder to develop it, and be prepared to value the process as much as the result, even if others do not see or understand its worth.

5. Hsü / Waiting (Nourishment)

Primary Trigrams

above *K'an* / The Abysmal, Water
below *Ch'ien* / The Creative, Heaven

Nuclear Trigrams

above *Li* / The Clinging, Fire
below *Tui* / The Joyous, Lake

There are two aspects to the times represented by this hexagram. The first is connected to the idea of water in the sky (*K'an* and *Ch'ien*). Rain will come (*K'an* has a naturally descending motion while *Ch'ien* naturally ascends) and with it all the blessings it brings, but it will come in its own time. To a large extent we have lost touch with the simple fact of our absolute dependence on rain. Waiting for it symbolizes that state of uncertainty that pertains when our very lives and livelihoods are at stake.

Waiting without any guarantee of relief is extremely uncomfortable and unpleasant for human beings. While we are rarely as much in control of events as we like to think, our culture does encourage us in the illusion that the direction and success or failure of our lives lies in our own hands and waiting destroys this fantasy, evoking restlessness, anxiety, and even depression. At such a time it is important to maintain a realistic view of the situation and of our resources, both inner and outer, neither denying the difficulties of the time nor becoming overwhelmed by them. Each moment offers us a choice: can we live creatively and joyously in the present – the only time we ever really have – or are we blinded to this moment and its fullness by our obsessive focus on the future and the hoped-for resolution of this time of waiting? This hexagram reminds us of these questions and the nuclear trigrams *Li*, symbolizing clear-sightedness, and *Tui*, meaning joy (as well as social intercourse such as conversation and the sharing of food and drink), indicate the path we should seek while we wait.

The second idea is related to the association of danger with *K'an*. If there is danger ahead then it is as well if we wait, or pause, at least, considering how best to use our strength to withstand it. In Hamlet's final words before the denouement of the play, 'The readiness is all'.[1] If what we are preparing for is truly of profound importance and value, even if it is death or a highly risky undertaking, the greatest danger lies in a recklessly blind or arrogant attitude, for that will only increase the danger we are in by reducing our clarity of vision and unbalancing us. Wisdom lies in seeing ourselves – and the challenge with which we are faced – absolutely clearly.

Another reading of this hexagram might suggest that as we wait we should contemplate whether the way in which we are nourishing ourselves – mindfully or mindlessly – is consistent with our hopes for the future. By reflecting deeply on our role in the process, rather than ignoring it or considering that the 'rains' will or will not come, regardless of our behaviour, we are witness to a belief in a participatory, rather than a random, universe.

The Changing Lines

9/1st Sometimes we are ready to play our part in a process or undertaking that requires the participation of others, but they are not ready and we must wait. We may be able to exert a gentle influence on them, but we cannot force the pace of development. This is as true for the situation where the 'others' are different parts of oneself as it is if they are actually other people.

9/2nd If we find ourselves in the position of having to wait for a long period of time, particularly if the wait reflects an apparently decreasing likelihood of an undesirable event taking place, we may become inattentive, complacent, even careless. At all times we should cultivate an alert attunement to the requirements of the present moment and not jump ahead to the possibilities that lie in the uncertain future.

9/3rd When the situation we find ourselves in feels dangerously unstable, we naturally become restless, uneasy, eager to make a move. In fact, the best way forward is to simplify our lives in preparation for whatever follows, limiting what we do and say to that which is true and necessary. This conscientiousness will have a calming and centring effect, both physically and mentally, and will help to curb any tendency towards impulsiveness.

6/4th   When the tension that has been building up in a situation is at its height, we may need to effect some reduction of pressure. If this can be done harmlessly by enjoying a break or doing something completely different, then we may find we are able to return to the situation with a different attitude. Another approach is to address each issue that now arises at the moment it appears, so that it never builds to a climax. This is specifically not about trying to resolve or 'fix' deep-seated problems or antagonisms; in a sense it involves accepting them as irresolvable – a constant – and starting afresh. It may be that we have been anticipating something that was never going to happen.

9/5th   If there exists an ideal way to endure and benefit from times of uncertainty and waiting, then it would undoubtedly require us to consider the balance between firmness (that is, a disciplined approach in our day-to-day life to issues of expenditure of resources, the regular acknowledgement of the present circumstances as a necessary part of our personal journey, self-awareness practice to keep us alert and honest, and the conscious cultivation of whatever degree of gratitude or cheerfulness we can manage without falsity) and, on the other hand, openness, surrender to what 'is', to not knowing, to life.

6/top   Containing our impatience or anxiety and enduring uncertainty is a tremendous challenge and requires courage and a high degree of consciousness. Maintaining calm in the face of the unknown is not only a remarkable achievement for the individual, it also provides a quiet centre of strength and wisdom for others. The 'ripples' that emanate from such a person travel a great distance in every direction. If we cannot imitate them, we can at least make the conscious choice to look to their example when we feel beset by uncertainty and stress.

Note

1. Quotations from *Hamlet* and *The Tempest* are from *The New Penguin Shakespeare* editions.

6. Sung / Conflict

Primary Trigrams

above *Ch'ien* / The Creative, Heaven
below *K'an* / The Abysmal, Water

Nuclear Trigrams

above *Sun* / The Gentle, Wood, Wind
below *Li* / The Clinging, Fire

Conflict is inevitable and unavoidable in life. It is the strength of the conflicting forces of the opposites that drives our growth forward, as individuals and as a culture. We find solutions that work for a time and then the characteristic pull or drive of an apparently opposite energy begins to undermine that balance and the process starts again. But this dynamic is full of life; it is the very stuff of life. The conflict that is addressed in this hexagram may be more deathly in its grip. If we are called upon to make choices or mediate between antagonistic and even apparently irreconcilable principles or individuals or goals, we must recognize that a possible outcome will be open conflict, the resolution of which is impossible to predict. When attitudes have hardened and there is such a core lack of 'fit', compromise may become unachievable. In such a case we must be prepared to concede that the barriers to resolution are insurmountable and retreat may be the only option.

How can we proceed short of this ultimate choice? The first steps are indicated by the nuclear trigrams *Sun*, the Gentle, and *Li*, the Clinging, Fire. We must work with what has hardened inside ourselves and gently open and investigate it. This process will lead to much greater clarity, which will serve us in dealing with the outer situation as well as the inner. Once we are quietly clear about where we stand ourselves, we can afford to be open to the other (indicated by the 'open', or 'empty' middle line of *Li*), to take in the point of view or needs that they feel to be under threat or challenge. If this does not lead to any softening of the conflict, then we can leave it without feeling we have failed or been defeated.

It is often true that if a 'third' position, principle, goal, or way can be found that both parties to the conflict honour and would place above or before their quarrel, then this common ground may be strong enough to overcome instinctive differences and make it possible to establish harmony. Further, a third person, somebody not emotionally involved, is often able to mediate between two parties to a conflict where they cannot make any headway themselves. We may find such a person outside the conflict, an individual whose judgement is respected by both parties; or we may find that we ourselves have an inner 'judge', a wiser and less partial self capable of seeing beyond the question of 'winning' or 'losing' and able to discern the choice that is most truly healing.

If we find that we are frequently faced with situations in which conflict arises, we should reflect on the choices we are making.

The Changing Lines

6/1st   We must not be naïve concerning the effects of our actions on others. Inexperience or a lack of worldliness may account for our clumsiness at times, but at other times it is due to a lack of forethought and consideration for the feelings of others. Rarely is offence taken without there being some grounds for it.

9/2nd   Ideally, all processes and energies move in a complementary way in relation to each other, tempering the polarities, balancing the extremes. However, at times this is far from the case, and we find ourselves and others unable to value and benefit from difference. We cannot find a common language at all. When the firm can become a bit more yielding and the yielding can accept a degree of firmness, the way forward will become clear.

6/3rd   The third position opens the interface between the protagonists in the conflict addressed in this hexagram. In situations of direct confrontation we may be tempted to surrender if we feel intimidated or unsure of our strengths. We make peace, but in truth nothing has changed in our attitude. A better choice would be to stand back, pause, and seek clarity, or simply to go our separate ways.

9/4th   The fourth position shares the conflictual interface with the third. Sometimes we may convince ourselves that we are ready to seek common ground when, on a deeper level, we are actually rigidly fixed in our position or full of barely conscious prejudice. Gentleness penetrates where hardness merely intensifies resistance and misunderstanding. We need to be utterly honest with ourselves before we 'throw the first stone'.

9/5th   Sometimes resolution of a conflict is much closer than we imagine; if we do our best to embrace both sides without seeking a premature resolution, the passage of time will do the rest. Jung observed that we outgrow most conflicts rather than resolve them. This may be hard to believe when we are in the midst of the suffering that accompanies any serious conflict, but, if we put our effort into staying in place, seeking understanding and remaining quietly true to ourselves, less harm will be done all around.

9/top   The top line represents a position from which we can review what has passed – or view what is still happening – and learn. Reflecting on this time of struggle we may find that, in spite of our best efforts, there has been no real change; we may even have worn ourselves out in fighting a battle we never could win. Perhaps we did not recognize the depths of the conflict, in which case it may resurface later. Perhaps we were trying heroically to deal with a situation on our own where we would have done better to enlist some help. For the present, the important thing may be simply to look after our immediate needs.

7. Shih / The Army

Primary Trigrams

above *K'un* / The Creative, Heaven
below *K'an* / The Abysmal, Water

Nuclear Trigrams

above *K'un* / The Receptive, Earth
below *Chên* / The Arousing, Thunder

This hexagram represents what lies deep inside the earth, or what is deeply a part of all of humanity, or what lies hidden in the individual. It addresses the question of resources, whether and how they can be called upon, and encourages us to consider what else may lie buried or unattended to within ourselves. *K'an* symbolizes groundwater, and *K'un* is the earth. It is seen in the *I Ching* as the army, because it is the strength and force that lies, ready to be called upon, in the general population. In this image, the one firm line in the second position is seen as the commander of the army, rightly positioned among his 'men', but we can also view it as representing the gifts or experiences or 'thing' that has real substance within us but that has become blocked or disregarded or inaccessible over time, unmourned, unused, unacknowledged. *K'an* represents a deep gorge or chasm with water rushing through; it also signifies danger and, as it is associated with the heart, it points to sorrow as well.

When we begin to explore or evoke these hidden depths/ resources we must do so with an intelligent and informed attitude. It would be a foolish commander who unleashed an army without preparing them and his plans. In the same way, when we are bringing to consciousness hidden feelings or experiences, we need to do so with as great a degree of awareness and preparedness as the military commander and not embark recklessly on a journey that may be long and difficult. Above all, we must not attempt to break down or disregard any resistance we encounter. *K'un* represents our inheritance as human beings, that which we all share, our common humanity. In its unconscious form in the individual or in the world it is powerful but inchoate, and, as with the army, if such forces are mishandled or manipulated it can lead to dangerous consequences.

The Changing Lines

6/1st   The times addressed by this hexagram may provide us with the opportunity – or the challenge – to learn something of our unknown 'face', those aspects or gifts that, like the dark side of the moon, have been invisible to us but of whose presence we may now have brief glimpses or intuitions. If we are to become acquainted with and own these new energies we must be prepared to take the time to connect with them personally and with feeling. There is no need to 'do' something with or about what is revealed; it is enough to clear a space for it to become what it will, to remain in relationship with it.

9/2nd   This strong line represents the hidden resource or the true flow of the personality. Whatever we undertake, on whatever scale, this element must be placed at its heart. Even if the course it is suggesting appears dangerous, it will provide the most reliable guide for how to proceed. At times we may lose track of where we were going or for what purpose, and at those times we serve ourselves best if we remain quietly open, calm and attentive.

6/3rd   If we remain receptive and trust the energy of that which wants to be recognized and grow within us, there is nothing to fear. Life is about the movement of forces possessing a tremendous capacity for perseverance and endurance. Our tendency to want to tame such energies, to 'prune' or restrict their growth, betrays our unease with their tenacity and apparent wilfulness.

6/4th   If we find ourselves confused about what is happening and what resources are available, it can help to pause and take stock of the balance of energies around and within us and how they are moving. We may still be 'geared up' for a struggle when that is no longer necessary; there may be a new possibility that we have yet to take into consideration; we may ourselves need something – rest, food, information. Paying attention to the flow of these different moods and movements can help us discern the next step.

6/5th   Those who are deeply aligned with the flow of life, the Tao, seem to do little yet accomplish much. If we are not attuned in this way, we may feel we are doing a lot and accomplishing little. If we find ourselves exhausting our limited resources, we should stop and consider if we have lost our connection to the simplicity reflected in the lines below.

> Who can by stillness, little by little
> make what is troubled grow clear?
> Who can by movement, little by little
> make what is still grow quick? [Le Guin, 1997]

6/top   The greatest resource of all lies in the energy of life and its desire for more of itself. While the forms it takes may vary, the hunger is constant. However, personally we experience many endings in life and we need to learn how to face them and complete the work they require before moving on. In this way we will not be carrying unnecessary 'baggage' into the next stage of our journey.

8. Pi / Holding Together (Union)

Primary Trigrams

above *K'an* / The Abysmal, Water
below *K'un* / The Receptive, Earth

Nuclear Trigrams

above *Kên* / Keeping Still, Mountain
below *K'un* / The Receptive, Earth

There are two strands to the picture at this time: the waters of the earth, represented by *K'an*, flow naturally to the sea. Water flows to water, and water obeys the drawing force of the moon (also *K'an*) through the tides. Thus, the yielding elements of water hold together through the natural laws governing gravity and tides. Against this natural background and its laws, the *I Ching* addresses the situation within the human world and, in particular, the requisite qualities for leadership that would enable one to command the respect and following of others, in the same way as the laws of nature command the movement of the waters. Those who wish to attain a position of influence in the eyes and hearts of others must first develop inner coherence and integrity; they must 'hold together' within themselves. And so the question of how to become a leader of others quickly becomes the question of how to lead one's own life. In other words, this hexagram throws us back upon ourselves in the way a Zen *koan* might do, challenging us to a deeper and more searching confrontation and questioning of our motives and desires, a more profound understanding of our true goals and ambitions.

Returning to the image drawn from the natural world, it is helpful to consider the principle of affinity. Water seems to seek water and all waters unify in the sea. The rush of great rivers to reach this self-fulfilling and self-annihilating goal can be breathtaking. Often we resist the pull of affinity or confuse it with other urges; on the one hand, it is frightening to align oneself with a powerful flow, while on the other, we long to identify with something larger than ourselves, even to subsume our identity in a 'greater' cause.

These reflections continually lead us back to the central juxtaposition of the 'many', represented by the yielding lines of lower primary trigram *K'un*, Earth and humanity, and the 'one', the single firm line in the fifth place, the position of the ruler of the hexagram. Whether and how we align ourselves with that to which we are drawn, whether and how we act as a magnet for those who are drawn to us, we have a responsibility to consider our position and actions with care and honesty.

The Changing Lines

6/1st   Within the structure and imagery of the hexagram, this line lies at the greatest distance from the strong 'magnetic' line in the fifth position. This might reflect the situation when we do not really feel strongly drawn towards anything or anybody and rather wish that we did. Everywhere we look seems more or less equally uninteresting. We have lost connection with ourselves at this point and the challenge lies in taking this sense of loss seriously and committing ourselves anew to the journey of discovery and self-awareness. Recognizing that we have lost our 'point of balance' (see the lines with which the Introduction opens), often brings a sense of relief and reconnection; at least we are on track again.

6/2nd When we least expect it – or under the most unlikely circumstances – we may find ourselves swept up by strong feelings or convictions, attracted to a person or idea that electrifies us. All such connections have much to teach us, whether they bear fruit or not. If we hold back out of fear of such powerful energies, we learn little. If we allow the flow to carry us mindlessly and then toss us aside at a later stage, we also may not learn much. There is a balance to be struck between allowing and staying alert.

6/3rd In a childlike way we may imagine that when the 'right' thing or person comes along it will be obvious and will hardly involve any decision at all. This is rarely true. Conflict is part of life and drives us forward; doubt encourages us to reflect and weigh up different possibilities. What works for us as individuals is something we learn through experiencing what doesn't work, and through taking responsibility for our choices.

6/4th   It is easy to confuse the search for others who share our goals or have similar likes or dislikes with the search for life-long soulmates or fellow travellers. It can be a relief to discover that a more limited connection can be fulfilling and afford much pleasure as well as providing the next step towards a longer-term commitment, either personal or spiritual. We do not have to figure it all out at once; nor do all our choices have to be 'forever'.

9/5th   This firm line gives the hexagram its title; it represents the element that holds all others together, the force of affinity or attraction. It may also represent the ego strengths that we build up during the course of life that enable us to survive – and even thrive – in the world. Taking this idea a step further, as we move through life the balance may shift towards a deeper sense of identity that becomes our guide. From time to time we may lose track of this centring force and have to bear not knowing what is holding us together at all. Perhaps it is just these times that begin to consolidate the sense of an inner guide.

6/top   Finding that we have missed out on the excitement of a particular time can lead to resentment and envy, particularly if it is the result of choices we made knowingly. When we are faced with acknowledging our isolation and discomfort in this way, it is better for us to aim for acceptance and clarity rather than immediately seeking to make good the lack. Perhaps we did not miss that much, or it was not that important, or we will know better for the next time. Some lessons are best learnt in solitude.

9. Hsiao Ch'u / The Taming Power of the Small

Primary Trigrams

above *Sun* / The Gentle, Wind, Wood
below *Ch'ien* / The Creative, Heaven

Nuclear Trigrams

above *Li* / The Clinging, Fire
below *Tui* / The Joyous, Lake

For better or worse, it is a time when a small or 'slight' element or force is holding a much greater energy in check. There are many ways this could work: something small and 'shadowy' preventing the great thing from proceeding; or, perhaps, although everything appears to be in order and ready, yet the time is not really 'right'; we must still wait, just a bit, or get one more thing ready. The influence of this element works to restrain an action or an energy, not to create an action of its own. In this case, the power of the Creative is being restrained as it seeks to rise and express itself fully.

This is a hopeful hexagram: even the 'slight', the 'yielding', at a particular time, can have an effect, and its power is through gentleness. As conscientious and peace-loving individuals have shown throughout time, sincerity, persistence, equanimity – a small word or gesture – can have far-reaching consequences. We should never underestimate the power of the small; like the wind, its influence may travel far.

We need to pay attention to details at such a time, attending to what is small and apparently insignificant, not overlooking it or thinking it unimportant. *Li*, representing fire and vision and clear-sightedness, reflects the importance of understanding the forces at work within and without, looking at the situation fearlessly. The 'small' element here may be welcome or not, but recognizing and addressing its presence, provenance, and power is likely to require both determination and honesty. The name of the hexagram is 'The Taming Power of the Small', not 'The Obstructing Power of the Small', and the choice of adjective reflects the attitude of respect that we need to bring to this effort of understanding.

Finally, the position of *Tui*, representing joy, should be noted. It lies within the hexagram, within the situation, and, if unrestrained, it would naturally rise. The presence or absence of joy and its quality or resonance in this situation may indicate where the restraining influence is at work.

The Changing Lines

9/1st   If, early on, we are able to recognize whatever it is that is holding us or the situation back and to understand the purpose it might be serving, we can align ourselves with this element or with the particular energy it represents and not waste our time in struggling against it. Eagerness and strength are wonderful qualities with which to embark on a course of action, but at times we need to exercise our insight and intuition concerning the details upon which we might be basing our future vision. If we take this time to honestly reconsider our plans in the light of what we have learnt through reflection, the whole situation may become more clear and free.

9/2nd   Our choices are affected by our relationships, whether in the past or in the present; in turn, those relationships may well be affected themselves, for better or for worse. Either way, it is not a time to act in an impulsive or conditioned way without thought for the wider influence we might have. We need to cultivate awareness, honesty, and the patience to consider the consequences of our actions for all those concerned.

9/3rd   Sometimes, when we feel we are being pressured into a decision, we automatically contract our attention to focus on what seems most demanding. By so doing we may become inattentive to details that appear too small to matter. If we become aware of this happening we can counteract it by pausing and consciously considering the possibility of other viewpoints. Opportunities for coming together with others may be lost if our minds are made up too quickly.

6/4th Often we neglect to consider that we may ourselves be preventing movement, for better or for worse. The energies of the time may seem too powerful, and we have taken it upon ourselves to become a bulwark against sudden change; we may be holding a precarious balance in a situation that has become polarized. There are many reasons why such dynamics might arise. As long as we resist the situation as it is, it will not be free to adjust from within. We need to release our grip – without devaluing the role we have been playing – and recognize that it may be time for others to bear responsibility as well. Stepping back may allow everybody to be more creative.

9/5th Sometimes we withhold support for others who may be advocating a more restrained approach because we fear losing 'face' if we acknowledge the wisdom of their way. Those who are not threatened by other viewpoints have no need to insist on their superiority; they lose nothing by considering other options. In fact, everybody gains when those who have influence are both strong and open; the resourcefulness of all is available as a resource for all.

9/top Learning to 'tame' ourselves and our reactions is one of life's great lessons. Every time we do it we gain more awareness of what motivates us as well as increasing our understanding of how sound decisions should be made. There is always a balance to be struck between control and spontaneity. Some things are within our power to change and others are not. Beyond that, the achievement of a degree of equanimity, even cheerfulness, and the ability to let go and relax are accomplishments that are much to be desired.

10. Lü / Treading (Conduct)

Primary Trigrams

above *Ch'ien* / The Creative, Heaven
below *Tui* / The Joyous, Lake

Nuclear Trigrams

above *Sun* / The Gentle, Wind, Wood
below *Li* / The Clinging, Fire

This hexagram pictures the interplay between two energies of very different apparent strengths. *Tui*, representing the youngest daughter, the Lake and Joy, is following close behind *Ch'ien*, representing the father, Heaven, and the great energy of creativity. The eager and hungry energy of the young and 'feminine' bumps into the established power of traditional authority. Both are powerful and the methods or energies that they employ to get what they want could easily lead to a dangerous confrontation unless both conduct themselves in such a way that no real injury befalls either. For reasons connected with the attributes of *Tui* and *Ch'ien*, they are both associated with the tiger, a potent symbol not only in China but also around the world. In the Introduction, a poem was quoted in which the final reward of knowing the point of balance at any moment is that one can 'think in front of the tiger'. The tiger seems to stand for the great mystery of existence, all that strikes terror in our hearts as we approach it, but, also, all that gives the deepest meaning to life. In many ways we could see the tiger as symbolizing all that is most beautiful and ruthless about life and its desire for more of itself. In certain forms of the practice of T'ai Chi, the end of each section is marked by a move called 'Carry Tiger to the Mountain', when the arms are used almost as a scoop to gather up the imagined animal and carry him gently to the mountain. Through this practice one comes to the point that the tiger has been gentled – it has become part of oneself – and it can be carried to the Mountain, *Kên*, the mysterious place of beginnings and endings.

Taken from one perspective, this hexagram reflects the process of learning. Treading in the footsteps of those greater than we are is a way to emulate their behaviour and characteristics. Within this hexagram we find that both *Sun*, the eldest daughter, and *Li*, the middle daughter, have preceded *Tui*, and thus the interpretation of the hexagram as one concerning learning by example is demonstrated. The qualities of perseverance and clear-sightedness are represented by *Sun* and *Li* respectively, and, taken with *Tui*'s attribute of cheerfulness and enthusiasm, indicate the attitudes and qualities most necessary and appropriate for learning.

The power represented by the upper trigram, *Ch'ien*, cannot easily be threatened or compromised by that which follows or attempts to emulate it. As long as the leading force commands respect and deserves the authority with which it is endowed, tolerance of youth and enthusiasm is the best response, not rejection or harsh criticism. In this hexagram we find both a serious observation on the nature of power and the powerful and also a more gentle comment on the process of learning and general conduct. If our desire to learn and to deepen our experience is genuine, then we must observe those we admire carefully and tread with caution.

Finally, another perspective must be mentioned even though its implications may not be clear. The energy of *Tui* is rising and will, in time, oust whatever is represented by *Ch'ien*. *Tui* is a challenging trigram to interpret, as elusive as the reflections that might play over the surface of a lake – there and not there. And yet, in a way, it is the most human of the trigrams, not so much representing an archetypal energy such as wind or fire, earth or heaven, beginnings or endings, as picturing the limited container of a lake and the human emotion of joy. This is the force that is pressing upon Heaven at this time.

The Changing Lines

9/1st   The way in which we conduct ourselves at the outset of an undertaking influences the entire process. Balancing a strong and eager start must be the recognition that there are others who have much more experience, who might help us if we do not alienate them through arrogance or inappropriate competitiveness. It is also true that others who are closer to us in position may feel threatened by our evident desire to advance. We must not over-compensate in this direction and allow the feelings or reactions of others to shape our decisions unduly – this benefits nobody – but we do well simply to recognize that initial conditions and choices are highly sensitive. This is where the learning begins.

9/2nd   When we are not in a particularly strong or influential position, we do well to make ourselves and our goals relatively transparent or, at the very least, not to encourage ourselves in extravagant visions that rely on a degree of manipulation or guile in order to succeed. At all times the more self-aware we can be, the less likely it is that we will become overwhelmed when events take unexpected turns or others disappoint us. A quiet heart and a willingness to learn and to move with the times create the best conditions for growth.

6/3rd   There are moments of encounter that affect us profoundly. If we are able to channel our 'hunger' into an eagerness to engage and understand, to align ourselves with the Other, whether inner or outer, rather than trying to challenge or defeat it, the opportunities for co-operation and creativity may develop rapidly. This is not the same as confusing ourselves with the Other or trying to become the Other. We need to acknowledge and work with both our limitations and our particular gifts, to neither deny nor overestimate either.

9/4th   It is not always possible to distinguish the teacher from the student or to locate with any certainty where an obstacle to communication lies. As a rule, if we find ourselves hardening in our minds or heart against a particular idea or person, then we would do well to consider if there is a way of becoming 'softer'. This is not the same as capitulating to them; rather, it creates the conditions for openness and a greater understanding of the true situation.

9/5th   Even when we find ourselves in a position of relative strength or stability, it is always wise to cultivate an ongoing awareness of how one's behaviour and choices seem to be affecting others or the situation in general. Clarity of vision (which means seeing what is actually there, not ignoring reality and not embellishing it) enables us to continually assess and respect our own characteristics and qualities as well as those of others. It also keeps us aware of, and grounded in, the requirements of the times.

9/top   In the end we do well to align ourselves with the energies that represent life and its continual renewal and regeneration. There is no other compass point that will direct us in as true and enduring a manner.

11. T'ai / Peace

Primary Trigrams

above *K'un* / The Receptive, Earth
below *Ch'ien* / The Creative, Heaven

Nuclear Trigrams

above *Chên* / The Arousing, Thunder
below *Tui* / The Joyous, Lake

This is a calendar hexagram representing February–March, the first month in the Chinese calendar. Within the hexagram the energies of the light and the dark are equal, but it is the light that is growing, from the bottom up, and the dark that is decreasing as it leaves from the top of the hexagram. Thus, the balance reflected in the lines is purely formal and does not necessarily signify equality. The image of an hourglass – albeit an inverted one – may be useful where half the sand has passed through and half remains. The movement is in one direction; the momentum is unstoppable; none the less, in the beginning this movement may be almost imperceptible. So it is with any change: the seeds may be invisible, its early growth may be unremarkable, but at a certain point it becomes both visible and undeniable.

In terms of the seasons, winter is releasing its grip. It is a time of year that can test both patience and trust, a time when doubt and limitation can lead to confusion and frustration. As the days lengthen the first real signs of change occur, but it may still be a long time before spring arrives. Sometime during this month the festival of Mardi Gras takes place, depending on when Easter falls. While this is a Christian celebration, instinctively it is not hard to imagine that its roots extend back to much earlier times, as it meets a need that has arisen out of the months of hardship and waiting. Pent-up energies express themselves in this festival of abandon and the celebration of the sensual.

The name of the hexagram is 'Peace', and this reflects the balance of the Creative (*Ch'ien*) and the Receptive (*K'un*). Most importantly, the forces of creativity are below and supporting the forces of receptivity, not at odds with them. Receptivity is elevated by this structure and creativity is rooted in the earth of common humanity. At this time of year our senses are heightened and we often experience a restlessness that seeks expression. We may naturally engage in a 'spring-clean', removing clutter from our surroundings, rearranging the furnishings, perhaps making an inventory of our possessions or our plans. The exhilaration we feel when we allow our energy to flow into such activities is explained by the fact that we have aligned ourselves with the deepest movements of the season. It feels good to order and simplify in preparation for a time of maximum growth. It goes without saying that this 'season' may occur at any time in our lives.

The hexagram presents us with images and associations that may challenge our ideas about peace and balance. There is nothing static about this view of peace. The energies of Shiva and Shakti, in their world-creating and world-destroying embrace, convey the dynamic of this time, as do the words of T. S. Eliot, 'Between melting and freezing / The soul's sap quivers' (Eliot, 1963, 'Little Gidding').

The Changing Lines

9/1st   Ability and determination are not always enough to assure growth. The capacity to sustain an effort, in the face of obstacles, without losing heart – even when progress is immeasurably slow – is a great gift. In accepting challenges we open ourselves to, rather than hardening ourselves against, the difficulties encountered. Time plays an essential role in any process: the time required may test us; it may also support us, and, in the end, it may provide an opportunity for others to join us.

9/2nd Balancing different needs and agendas sometimes requires us to adopt a low profile, to keep our counsel and cultivate patience and awareness. This is not the same as withdrawing or opting out. Our responsibility as a participant in, and witness to, the times does not cease when all seems to be well, or when our particular role seems to be less important than that of others.

9/3rd At the growing edge of change we might be tempted to either over- or underplay our hand, to push our advantage unnecessarily, or to hesitate and draw back. This is more likely to happen when we experience a shift in the conditions to which we have become accustomed, enabling us to progress more rapidly. We might race ahead unwittingly or compensate by drawing back. All we need do, in fact, is become aware of the change and consciously make whatever adjustment is required.

6/4th There can be a feeling of power and exhilaration when everything seems to be going well. If this tips over into a sense of invulnerability, then the dynamic balance of the times may become too personally charged. All increase is followed by decline, but if there is no external restraint or obvious limitation, then we must recall and remember this natural fact ourselves and embody the wisdom of balance.

6/5th At times, rather than trusting in the natural movement of the time, we make our own move prematurely, based on the feeling that our position is strong. When we pre-empt the natural flow in this way we may find ourselves checked by events beyond our control and we must then be content to wait and see what the consequences of our choice will be. Now the patience and balance that we were unable to sustain earlier is essential. While we wait we would do well to review our actions and seek understanding and clarity.

6/top Discernment and inner balance are vital when the conditions within which we have been operating are undergoing fundamental change. If we can remain quiet and centred, we will be in the best possible position to judge where we might be called upon to play a part in the new situation. The combination of concentration and creativity is a powerful one.

12. P'i / Standstill

Primary Trigrams

above *Ch'ien* / The Creative, Heaven
below *K'un* / The Receptive, Earth

Nuclear Trigrams

above *Sun* / The Gentle, The Penetrating, Wind, Wood
below *Kên* / Keeping Still, Mountain

This is a calendar hexagram representing the seventh month of the Chinese calendar, August–September, a period that concludes with the autumn equinox. The order of the trigrams in the previous hexagram, *T'ai* / Peace, is reversed and instead of the ascending movement of Heaven supporting the descending movement of Earth, here the two draw apart and the creative conjunction that heralds spring is apparently broken. The light lines that filled the hexagram three months ago, at the time of the spring solstice (see Hexagram 1, *Chi'en* / Heaven) have now lost half their strength. The energies of growth and increase are declining and the balance will now begin to shift towards those of retreat and decay.

While this lessening of the light is to be expected in the natural cycle of the seasons and can even be welcomed and enjoyed, the hexagram also points to the more human experience of disjointedness and lack of 'fit', the feeling that the tide is out, or, at the very least, and perhaps more alarmingly, it is ebbing. At such a time nothing seems to flow easily; we feel helpless and unsettled and may be tempted to act impulsively in an attempt to detoxify the atmosphere. The nuclear trigrams suggest that gentleness (*Sun*) and stillness (*Kên*) may be a better way of managing frustration; a quiet heart at such a time is a great help while considering what else might be done. Perhaps it is time to do a sort of inner (and, possibly, outer) inventory, to 'put our house in order'. The story of the

Rainmaker is a good example of this: in an area in China in which there had been little or no rain for a long time the villagers, fearing for their crops and animals, sent for the Rainmaker. When he arrived, the old man asked for a small hut on the edge of the village in which he might stay. For a week he was hardly seen and, at the end of the week, it began to rain. Full of gratitude, the villagers asked him what he had done. His reply was that he had slept when he was tired, eaten when he was hungry, fetched wood when he wanted a fire, drawn water when he was thirsty. In other words, he aligned himself with his own Tao and by thus ordering his own being internally, he became a centre of external order and the 'out of joint' state in nature corrected itself. The trigram *K'un* represents an 'earthed' state of quiet carefulness in expenditure of money or energy, and this is not dissimilar to the actions of the Rainmaker.

Finally, considering the primary trigrams of *Ch'ien* and *K'un* gives us a picture of these two great energies essentially 'out of synch'; there is no area of overlap, no common ground. If we find ourselves in the situation where our most central energies are opposed or unconnected, then we need to reflect on how (or if) we can realign them, get them working together rather than against each other, like two horses pulling in the same direction rather than engaging in a tug of war. It may not be possible to do so at present, in which case it will be of benefit to recognize and accept that 'fact'.

The Changing Lines

6/1st   At a time of disconnection or disorientation we cannot afford to be naïve, on the one hand, or to allow ourselves to be provoked into rash or idealistic gestures on the other. We must learn to sit with discomfort and uncertainty and accept them as a natural part of the cycle of life. A quiet yet attentive attitude prepares us to respond flexibly to whatever happens next.

6/2nd   Feeling frustrated or trapped by circumstances, we are in danger of worsening our conflict if we choose to act recklessly. Similarly, reverting to a childlike helplessness, from which we turn towards an inappropriate parent figure, will only prolong the trying times. The only helpful response is to accept things as they are and then try to gain some insight into the nature of the energies at work.

6/3rd If no useful connections can be made and progress seems to be halted, then we do well to accept we have gone as far as we can go for the present. This ability to step back and realistically appraise a situation is not the same as admitting defeat. In fact, we strengthen our judgement and enable the flow of events to be restored through our non-resistance to what exists.

9/4th At times, feelings of confusion and powerlessness can be used as signals that we need to get another perspective on what we are perceiving as standstill. We may even be contributing unwittingly to the continuation of the situation. Seeking a sense of the wider context within which we are acting may open our eyes and enable us to understand the nature of the energies at work at a much deeper level. It may be that we will then be in a position to help and guide others.

9/5th Just when it seems that order is being restored and the danger has passed, we may relax prematurely, 'take our eye off the ball'. If we mistake part of the picture – that which seems strong and 'full' – for the whole, we could almost believe that every aspect is equally promising. The very nature of the time represented by this hexagram is that it is still bright and strong in one area, but that area is being diminished by the ascending darkness. There is work to be done while there is still the light to do it. We prune trees at this time of year to guarantee strong shoots in the spring; the wise person does likewise.

9/top The conditions represented by this hexagram are coming to a close. Rather than remain isolated, as it is easy to become when personal experience is as uncomfortable as it has been, it is now time to join up with others, perhaps even to share what has been learnt or gained through the time of dislocation. As in the story of the Rainmaker (above), at this point personal behaviour may have universal effects.

13. T'ung Jên / Fellowship

Primary Trigrams

above *Ch'ien* / The Creative, Heaven
below *Li* / The Clinging, Fire

Nuclear Trigrams

above *Ch'ien* / The Creative, Heaven
below *Sun* / The Gentle, Wind, Wood

There is a great simplicity at the heart of this hexagram, reminding us of our common humanity. The image is of fire under the open skies of heaven. Over the millennia, human beings have come together and found fellowship around fires. In a sense, we could consider these gatherings – and the more general mastery of fire – as the earliest expression of human culture. Stories were told, dances performed, plans made, disputes aired and settled. The reality of community was demonstrated, validated, and witnessed by all around the fire. This hexagram directs our attention to the fact that this coming together of individuals is not to be a hidden or secretive affair; the strength of a body of people who openly celebrate their fellowship resides in mutual respect and in the absence of dark motives or liaisons that invariably lead to inner divisions. The time, then, may be one in which the individual is seeking, or needs to seek, this sort of fellowship, perhaps as a way to move beyond narrower personal constraints, obstacles, or fears.

Throughout life we alternate between finding or making our meanings primarily on our own and working things out through our interactions with others. Some of us will always prefer the former – the individual path – and some will naturally seek the latter. Whatever our natural inclination, there is a warmth and connectedness to be found in open fellowship without which we can become isolated, out of touch, and a bit 'chilly'. None the less, we must also be cautious; there are times when feelings of loneliness may make us vulnerable to those who would offer an apparently appealing and immediate solution; our desire to be part of some fellowship may drive us to join up with any fellowship. It is not a time to allow emotions to lead the way; we need to be clear-eyed and attuned to our intuition, then we will sense whether or not we can share in the fellowship offered in a wholehearted and sincere way.

The Changing Lines

9/1st   Sometimes we find ourselves in the position of feeling we must ally ourselves with one group or another at a time when we are simply not gathered enough in ourselves to make a wise choice. Rarely is this sense of urgency borne out by events, and it is far better for all if we can pause and review what it is that we are truly seeking before making a decision that we may soon regret. Decisions taken impulsively or reactively frequently require us to back down at a later date when we are able to see more clearly.

6/2nd   Not surprisingly, tolerance of difference and openness to new ideas and views is often directly connected to richness of exchange. When fellowship becomes exclusive, prescriptive and in-bred, we cannot risk transparency and we become, instead, guarded and mistrustful of others. Such a fellowship will soon break down, as its usefulness is limited.

9/3rd   At times we may feel under considerable pressure, from within or without, to 'jump' in a particular direction, and it could be tempting to disregard a less clamorous part of ourselves that is quietly in touch with a different sense of how – or on what basis – our choices should be made. We need to learn to recognize when we are caught up by an exciting but unreal urgency and to deliberately make the choice to step back and reflect rather than act.

9/4th   Not uncommonly, we attempt to escape from unsatisfactory relationships by seeking new ones before we have dealt with the issues and feelings associated with the old ones. We only perpetuate dysfunctional patterns of relating if we avoid engaging honestly with each other and ourselves. It might be appropriate for us to move on from current partnerships or fellowships, but the clearer we can be about why, and why now, the greater will be the chance that our next choice is a wise one. The questions we might need to ask ourselves at such a moment will not find easy answers; they should form the basis for an unhurried and gentle reflection on issues of autonomy, inclusion, and motivation.

9/5th   When we are most visibly associated with, and integral to, a particular group or viewpoint it can be almost impossible to allow ourselves to doubt, to open ourselves to radically different possibilities or movements of energy, to rethink everything. Yet, if we are capable of this act of faith in Life itself, and if we can release personal fears and goals and open ourselves to inspiration and to the present moment, then we may experience a transformation within our own lives and have a far-reaching effect on many.

9/top   There is a story about a man who dropped his keys in the street one evening. A passer-by offered to help when he saw the man searching in the circle of light under a street-lamp. Was that where they dropped? No, but he was looking there because that was where the light was better. It may be that for a long time we persist in looking in the 'wrong' place for fellowship; it is easier for us to look where it is 'light' and familiar than where it is 'dark' and unknown. It is never too late to learn.

14. Ta Yu / Possession in Great Measure

Primary Trigrams

above *Li* / The Clinging, Fire
below *Ch'ien* / The Creative, Heaven

Nuclear Trigrams

above *Tui* / The Joyous, Lake
below *Ch'ien* / The Creative, Heaven

This hexagram represents an ideal: it pictures a brilliant sun high in the sky and suggests this as a symbol for the individual whose great gifts are governed by clear vision and discerning judgement. It further suggests that this individual's outstanding qualities both reflect and create the exceptional nature of the times. Rarely do we encounter such a person; rarely do we identify ourselves as so gifted; rarely do we feel the situations of our lives to be so full of light and creativity. The interpretation of this imagery is not easy.

Li represents the eye – vision, awareness, perhaps consciousness – and it is this quality or capacity that is emphasized here, particularly in its role as a conduit of light and understanding to the other five lines and as a channel for their creative energies. What we see and how we name it shapes our judgement and our choices. It has been said, 'To see all is to forgive all'. The gifted individual pictured here has perhaps attained this level of wisdom, but our vision is much more likely to be partial, based on limited information, uncertain motives, or fleeting emotions. Harsh or ill-informed judgements may result in the limitation of our own creativity or that of others. The times may offer an important opportunity to take stock of how – or if – we are nurturing our unique gifts. To ignore or devalue our skills, our individual 'genius', is to deprive the world of our particular 'light'. To own and take responsibility for those skills, to 'possess' them, requires that we withdraw projections we may have made on to others regarding their gifts and responsibilities and that we devote ourselves, in all humility, to the quiet work of clarifying and refining our gifts.

Finally, we talk about 'seeing things in a particular light' when we mean that our vision and, therefore, our judgement, is being shaped or focused in a particular way. While we cannot remove ourselves and our subjectivity from the act of seeing, it is useful if we can identify how and why we are choosing to see in any one 'particular light' rather than in another. If we cannot identify this for ourselves, others may be able to enlighten us.

The Changing Lines

9/1st   We all possess gifts, and the ideal early environment would both recognize those gifts and nurture them without pressuring the individual to perform before they are ready to do so. Some among us are particularly gifted; still, time is required for the maturation of both the person and the gift. If we confuse our gift with ourselves we may lay claim to it in a personal way and use it to increase our self-esteem. When we are able to value what we have been given and nurture and share it responsibly, then the gift serves to enrich our own lives and those of others; it becomes part of the collective treasury.

9/2nd   The greatest 'possession' we have is our own unique inner light; its worth is unrelated to our social standing or apparent sphere of influence. We need to recognize and nurture this inner flame daily, developing a practice that affirms its beauty and follows its guidance. Inner 'voices' may mock or decry this practice, but it represents the only true path to wisdom. We learn patience, develop a compassionate and gentle attitude towards ourselves, and become altogether more forgiving and light-hearted.

9/3rd   Sometimes a parting of the ways is thrust upon us when we feel least ready to undertake responsibility for ourselves. We may have considered that as long as we followed what seemed to be the obvious path, we would be fine. But the very nature of our individual gifts is that they require us to recognize, nurture, and share them in a way that is peculiarly appropriate to them alone. If we fail to do this, sooner or later we will experience a real test of our commitment to self-awareness and the growth of wisdom. We can put it off for a long time, but not forever.

9/4th The practice of meditation or any disciplined reflective process can create a type of holding environment that not only restrains the impulsive use or waste of gifts but also transforms them from within. By yielding to this process we put ourselves and our gifts at the disposal of a greater intelligence, however we might individually think of such a power. There are many ways that we may temporarily convince ourselves that our choices and actions are serving others when they are essentially self-serving or opportunistic. The hardest choices generally are those that require us to detach ourselves from any particular outcome.

6/5th The *Tao Te Ching* emphasizes repeatedly the paradox of having through not-having, knowing through not-knowing, and the situation pictured in this hexagram is one in which the greatest gifts are possessed by the most open and empty individual. Inevitably, times change, and the rhythms of opening and closing, filling and emptying, expansion and contraction, overtake us and force us to realign our energies and renegotiate our balances. Life teaches us the importance of letting go over and over again.

9/top Natural cycles of growth and decline are affected only minimally by human intervention, yet at times we all subscribe to the illusion of control because the alternative is rather frightening. In fact, our strength lies in surrendering to, and working with, the flow of the times, rather than seeking to force or guarantee a particular outcome.

15. Ch'ien / Modesty

Primary Trigrams

above *K'un* / The Receptive, Earth
below *Kên* / Keeping Still, Mountain

Nuclear Trigrams

above *Chên* / The Arousing, Thunder
below *K'an* / The Abysmal, Water

Within the hexagram, all aspects of movement are in balance: the earth (*K'un*) sinks while the mountain (*Kên*) rises; thunder (*Chên*) rises while water (*K'an*) sinks. From this comes the familiar idea that the forces of nature equalize the heights of the mountains and the depths of the valleys over time, that water will carve and erode stone and fill every low-lying area and carry its burden of earth towards the sea to be deposited afresh along the way, recreating the land that will eventually rise again. The wise person recognizes that as we are a part of nature and its cycles and balancings, we do well not to over-value the heights of achievement or gain, or to fear excessively those times when our efforts fail to attract recognition or appreciation. In this hexagram, the emphasis is on the important balance between self-belief or self-confidence and something like reserve or – difficult word – humility. True modesty embraces this balance, and the image of a mountain beneath and within the earth is a powerful representation of this quality.

Modesty is not about denying or minimizing one's gifts or experience. It would seem that the acknowledgement of the inner 'mountain' carries with it, ultimately, a responsibility to use what is great in the service of all. (Not doing so, we risk becoming smug or self-satisfied, not open to renewal.) That which is great in us does not 'belong' to us, nor does it make any one person a better or more worthy person. A well-known Biblical observation says, 'Of those to whom much has been given, much will be required'. The Earth (*K'un*) is the grounding factor here: literally, it 'earths' the radiance, and, in a sense, it claims it for all of humanity. We cannot do anything about the equalizing forces in nature, but it is up to us to see that we act in harmony with these forces and do not hoard or squander our gifts, thus creating greater inequalities. The nuclear trigrams carry a balancing message themselves: *Chên*, representing action and strength of the will, as well as the strong initiating energy necessary for new beginnings, and *K'an*, representing the depths, the heart, the feeling function, and powerful deep energies. These are the forces that lie within the hexagram, and they indicate that modesty is not an easy attitude or pose but, rather, a measure of character. *Chên* could suggest an impulse towards self-serving choices and *K'an* might suggest a capitulation to whatever influence is exercising the greatest attraction at the moment. When issues of passion and power are activated by the times, the interests of all are best served by those who remain still and connected to humanity in its widest sense. It is in our own interest to tame those desires or ambitions that are born of fear and nurtured or fuelled by greed.

The Changing Lines

6/1st   Few of us are born modest; those who genuinely possess this quality are able to move freely without offending or challenging others, possibly on account of their relative transparency. We do not sense a hidden agenda and we tend to welcome the clarity they bring. By way of contrast, we generally recognize false modesty fairly quickly. Sometimes, an individual 'opts out' of cultural expectations or personal achievement out of fear or anger. In that case, their presence often feels troubled or heavy with grievance.

6/2nd   The interesting thing about a modest attitude is that it can support great achievements. When our efforts are heartfelt, yet we are not attached to a particular outcome, we are most likely to be able to take each step as it presents itself, whether as an obstacle or as an apparently free passage onward. If we feel we know where we want to end up, then we can become easily disheartened when our path takes us in a different direction. This attitude can also be applied to how we speak to ourselves or others about our goals: the greater the emphasis we place on the achievement of a particular goal, the more we create a 'hostage to fortune'; we may well conclude by considering ourselves a failure in our own and the eyes of others if our plans fail to be realized.

9/3rd   A time may come when we are faced with the choice of whether to allow our gifts more visibility or to effectively deny them by opting for invisibility. There is a saying, 'Use it or lose it', and such a moment may challenge us on that level. On the other hand, there are individuals for whom the choice to step back from greater visibility is genuine, reflecting their wish to remain simply connected to ordinary human beings and the rhythms of life. This is not false modesty, or an irritating unwillingness to recognize one's gifts, but is, rather, an authentic expression of a person who feels fulfilled by his life and content with his choices.

6/4th   As children and young adults we are encouraged to aim high, to forge a strong ego capable of rising to challenges, and to make a place for ourselves in the world. This is perfectly appropriate; however, a time comes when we have done our best and life seems to be asking for a different level of development, a different set of skills that have to be learnt afresh. It can be a trying time, and we do well to release our old methods and measures and seek new ways of being in the world, ways that allow for not-knowing and for learning through experience rather than having all the answers from the outset.

6/5th   The attribute of modesty can extend to our expectations of life as well as to our view of ourselves. If we feel life owes us a smooth journey, continuous health, and an enjoyable standard of living, we will most certainly be disappointed. If, on the other hand, we recognize that life is not easy, that loss and sadness are as much a part of it as are gain and happiness, then, when the natural challenges and obstacles of life present themselves, we are prepared to meet them with a quiet heart. The more rooted we are in the present moment, the better equipped will we be to learn from, and even enjoy, the experiences which come to us.

6/top Modesty is so highly prized by the Chinese that it is seen as the supreme virtue. It is true that a person who goes through life with genuinely modest expectations linked to an ability to enjoy and appreciate the many small blessings of life will probably grow old without resentment and with few enemies. But for many of us it has been much more of a struggle to stay quietly grounded, both within and without. For us, the achievement of a degree of peace and acceptance as we approach old age and death is the goal of our journey. In the end, wisdom supersedes modesty because it finds no fault and values all paths and all choices equally.

16. Yü / Enthusiasm

Primary Trigrams

above *Chên* / The Arousing, Thunder
below *K'un* / The Receptive, Earth

Nuclear Trigrams

above *K'an* / The Abysmal, Water
below *Kên* / Keeping Still, Mountain

Enthusiasm is an experience or feeling of excited 'fullness' or increase that invigorates and elevates us, making us feel more optimistic, more powerful, with more self-belief. We can infect others with our enthusiasm, drawing them to us, lifting them out of a heavier or narrower vision. In fact, without the co-operation of others, the energy of enthusiasm may fade or become more vulnerable to doubt. This complex relationship is reflected in the structure of *Yu* where five yielding ('Earth') lines and one firm ('Heaven') line are dynamically balanced. If we consider Earth as representative of mortality, the body, the transient forms of life and perhaps its more depressive energies, and Heaven as representative of the transcendent, the spirit, then the juxtaposition and interaction of these two at this particular moment is delicate, sensitive, yet full of potential for growth and creativity.

The nature of enthusiasm is such that it requires more of itself to keep going, to keep it 'bubbling' and fresh-feeling, otherwise its tendency is either to dissipate or to become disconnected from reality, from 'real' life. It must be harnessed, made human, grounded through choice and action, activities that may feel tedious – even deadly – at times. The earthing of enthusiasm may strip it of its energy or it may transform it into something far more enduring and powerful; the outcome will depend on the degree to which we commit ourselves to this transformation. The nuclear trigrams suggest an inner balance that will continue to give life and hope to the inspired energy of enthusiasm while we see the process through: *K'an* symbolizes the heart and the flow of our innermost being, that which is never halted for long, while *Kên* represents the mountain, stillness, and the quiet work of reflection.

Enthusiasm for an idea or project may be a strong preliminary indication of where our path lies, and recalling our initial enthusiasm may help sustain us further down that path. However, a tendency to cling to our enthusiasms and to resist examining them may lead to others behaving in a spoiling or destructive manner; they are doing the 'earthing' for us. Similarly, just when we want to instil enthusiasm in others, we may find that they seem alienated by our heady energy or simply totally resistant to it. Enthusiasm may have unexpected and surprising effects on others, and we should pause and be prepared rather than spilling out our ideas.

In spite of the complexities associated with enthusiasm, the lack of it can be deeply disheartening and distressing. Accepting this state of affairs rather than being drawn into a denial of it may require considerable courage and patience, but only through such acceptance will we remain quietly open and receptive to the first breath of new life when it comes.

Music and the uses and effects of music have been associated with this hexagram.

The Changing Lines

6/1st   At times we may be inspired by the energy and success of another person and feel encouraged to follow their example. At other times we may simply feel competitive or envious, begrudging them their achievement or minimizing it. Each of us has our own path to follow and we only undervalue our own or the other person's progress by comparing them. Generally, we make our task more difficult if we are using another person as a measure because motivation based on example can turn quickly to discouragement. However, at times we may be profoundly inspired (literally, in-spirit-ed) by the courage and integrity of another person, and the result can be a true deepening of our convictions and our capacity to persevere.

6/2nd We may follow the example of others enthusiastically for a period of time, and we may learn a great deal, particularly if we apply ourselves to that task, but sooner or later we will probably need to define our own path. Often this moment is signalled by a period of discontent or frustration that we may resist acknowledging, preferring instead to find fault in others. Eventually, the difference in energies or inclinations must be accepted, and then the situation is freed to flow naturally again. It may be that disagreements can be resolved, but it is more likely that we need to go our separate ways.

6/3rd Any undertaking in which we are engaged heart and soul will bring with it moments of real challenge, even crisis; we may suddenly feel deeply conflicted, exhausted, full of doubt, worn down by the obstacles we must continually face and overcome. At such a time our greatest need is for rest and a period of quiet. Even a few minutes of sitting quietly, breathing and allowing the body to settle, can make a difference. When we relocate the point of balance within in this way, we create a space in which our priorities may find a more natural balance as well. Adrenalin can keep us 'high' for a long time, but in the end, it is our quieter and more personal resources that must sustain us.

9/4th When we alone are responsible for providing the essential inspiration, drive, and vision that fuel an undertaking, then if we become tired, ill, or disheartened we may fear that all we have achieved so far will be lost. If our project is not supported by others, or if the pace we have set ourselves is unrealistic, then the loss of momentum may offer an opportunity to reflect on the whole process. On the other hand, by releasing the reins of control for a while we may find there are others who are willing and available to step in and who may bring an altogether different quality of energy with them.

6/5th The relationship of allies may change subtly, depending on circumstances, and those who were previously content to relinquish responsibility for leadership may find themselves moved to take a more active role at another time. Perhaps the original enthusiasm and motivation came from the vision of one individual, but others then pick up the spark and ensure that it becomes a flame. If a project is to realize its greatest potential we need to attract others to our cause: a tiny trickle of water will only reach the sea if it can join with other moving bodies of water.

6/top   Enthusiasm can become delusion if we allow ourselves to simply rise on the 'bubble' of its energy, imagining that it will continue indefinitely. It would be churlish not to enjoy it and foolish not to make the most of its possibilities, but wisdom lies in recognizing it as simply a part of the greater cycle of energies and opportunities coming together and then coming apart.

17. Sui / Following (Tracking)

Primary Trigrams

above *Tui* / The Joyous, Lake
below *Chên* / The Arousing, Thunder

Nuclear Trigrams

above *Sun* / The Gentle, The Penetrating, Wind, Wood
below *Kên* / Keeping Still, Mountain

Tui, standing in the west and representing autumn, withdraws from the hexagram while *Chên*, standing in the east and representing spring, enters and ascends. Between autumn and spring lies winter, present implicitly although not explicitly in this hexagram. *Tui* is also associated with the mouth, with speech, and is, therefore, a very 'human' trigram. Its energy is joyful, positive, but also changeable. As the lake reflects whatever passes over it, so *Tui* can represent fleeting moments of emotion. *Chên* represents the powerful initiating energy of spring and first growth as well as being the trigram associated with the oldest son, who was responsible for the observance of ritual. Taking all these attributes and associations into consideration, we might imagine that the times represented by this hexagram require decisive, enthusiastic action and communication. But within the hexagram lie two trigrams that suggest an altogether different approach: *Kên* represents stillness and introspection, while *Sun* is associated with gentleness and a more intuitive attitude. In somewhat the same way as winter is implied in this hexagram, these qualities too are hinted at or 'hidden'. Linking these two strands of interpretation together might suggest that attention should be paid to both the manifest and explicit realities of the time and also to what is not manifest but may be intuited or experienced through meditation or reflection. Bridging these two 'worlds' may be the challenge of the times.

A further image suggests itself as *Chên*, representing, in this case, thunder, rises towards *Tui*, the lake. Traditionally, thunder is considered to rest in this position and, taken with the other associations mentioned above, this emphasizes the importance of recognizing that rest, stopping, is as essential to life as moving and acting. As so often in life, this hexagram confronts us with contradictory images and impulses, the seen and the unseen, activity and rest, the apparent and the implied. The Chinese character that is the name of the hexagram is translated as 'Following'. In this case, following should not necessarily be taken to mean following somebody else's lead, but rather a sort of 'tracking' of the movements of energy within and without. If we cannot see what unites these opposites we may feel confused and rudderless, unsure of how best to align ourselves with the times and thus benefit from their particular gifts. It may be that we have been applying an inappropriate or outdated view of how things should be to a situation that is, as always, entirely new.

The Changing Lines

In each case the correspondence of the lines and the positions is appropriate, i.e., firm lines in firm positions and yielding lines in yielding positions. This is true conventionally of the first, second, fifth, and sixth lines, and it is true in a practical sense of the third and fourth lines which, although they do not agree with their position, are, none the less, apparently wise in being yielding in the critical third position and strong in the unobtrusive fourth position. However, as the lines change, representing an unseen or perhaps unconsidered possibility, the result is a clarification or resolution of previous inconsistencies or confusion. This reflects the theme suggested above and emphasizes the importance of patience, receptivity, and a capacity to think the unthinkable at such a time.

9/1st   Under ordinary circumstances, if we are clear in our intent, able and energetic, we would expect to see our goals accomplished, but under the circumstances portrayed in this hexagram, we might be better served by stepping back from the situation early on and cultivating a more open and discerning attitude, allowing ourselves – and events – to be gathered up and come together naturally. This does not mean abandoning our hopes or vision; it means not acting precipitously, remaining receptive to different voices and counsels and, perhaps, being prepared to join with others.

6/2nd Sometimes an unexpected alignment may occur when we depart from our customary view of ourselves or our influence. This may be signalled by a sense that things are falling into place or requiring less effort to sustain. It may also be that, by allowing our own flow to determine our choices rather than being moved by others, we find an altogether new energy and we attract others with whom we share important views or goals.

6/3rd While we may, at times, choose to keep a 'low profile' in order to gain time while the dynamics of a situation become clarified, we may also need to be aware of the desire to avoid conflict; often a confused picture is hiding a reality we would prefer not to recognize. Nothing creative can emerge until we allow ourselves to understand the true nature of the forces at work.

9/4th Sometimes, after an initial phase that draws on all our resourcefulness and enthusiasm, we find that everything begins to fall into place and flow quite effortlessly. It can be quite disconcerting and even disheartening when new obstacles appear. We have travelled quite a way from our point of departure, and the original vision that empowered us may have lost its force or we may ourselves have been changed through the process. The challenge is not to find a way back, but to discern the way forward. The dynamics now shift on to a different and deeper level.

9/5th In a position of authority we carry a treble responsibility: first, to those who look to us for leadership or guidance, second, to the greater movements and rhythms of the time, and third (perhaps most importantly), we must be responsible to ourselves, to our own path and vision. The presence or absence of overlap in these areas of responsibility may make our task easier or may make it much harder. The benefits of relinquishing personal influence may only become visible when we clear the way for a much more powerful surge of energy – one that we may have been blocking – to rise up and resonate at a higher level.

6/top Even when an ending seems imminent we have a role to play; it is a time when we can commit our work and its effect to higher energies, hoping that it will be a force for good as it leaves our hands and our sphere of influence. This can be done to even greater effect if we are able to acknowledge and take responsibility for both our positive and our negative contributions, not allotting blame, but simply owning our part. A strong spiritual and creative energy field will then embrace our work.

18. Ku / Work on What Has Been Spoiled (Decay)

Primary Trigrams

above *Kên* / Keeping Still, Mountain
below *Sun* / The Gentle, Wind

Nuclear Trigrams

above *Chên* / The Arousing, Thunder
below *Tui* / The Joyous, Lake

The wind (*Sun*) is trapped at the base of the mountain (*Kên*). It is not a momentary standstill of air that is being addressed, but rather a situation that has arisen in the past and continues. The natural circulation of air is represented by the nuclear trigrams *Chên*, symbolizing the vigorous movement of beginnings, thunder, storms, even earthquakes, and *Tui*, the joyous, associated with movement arising from enthusiasm. Applied to life, we see that that which cannot move and circulate without hindrance will, in time, stop growing and developing and begin to stagnate and decay. Whatever is preventing or inhibiting or corrupting our energies, disabling us and our capacity to move and express ourselves, needs to be recognized and released freely.

It is perverse but true that although we know that we only have the present in which to make choices and live our lives, we continue to be affected by, and even in thrall to, the past, repeating behaviour that causes us or others to suffer. Much of our conditioning occurred in a way that renders it inaccessible to examination or change, but we can at least recognize that we are a great deal more than that conditioning and not allow it to continue to inhibit and spoil our freedom of choice in the present. Some aspects of the past and their effects in the present are more accessible, but we need to be aware of the power of the past and our conditioning to draw us away from the only time we have to live in, Now. We can find ourselves trapped again if the focus of our desire to understand becomes identified with events or figures in the past; the crucial emphasis is on re-establishing the conditions for movement and joy to occur in the present.

In this hexagram we find that conditions that prevent the natural flow of life have taken hold. That recognition, in itself, may be enough to release the trapped energy, but, if not, then the limiting conditions must be identified, named, and recognized as belonging to the past and not to the present. A clear act of will is required to set aside old patterns and to become more aware and responsible, but sometimes we need first to remember where those old patterns began and why, and perhaps even to have somebody help us to do that work. Strong feelings may be evoked: understanding causes can easily lead to blame and the desire for retribution, but this only leads to the continuation of destructive patterns and does not help. Discriminating the important work from the more instinctive desires for revenge, on the one hand, or harmony, on the other, is essential.

While these comments have been considering the effects of the past on individuals, they apply equally to institutions. It is not at all unusual for such bodies to experience the stagnating and spoiling effects of ill-considered decisions or out-of-date patterns from the past that become real barriers to development and creativity in the present.

The Changing Lines

The commentaries on the changing lines emphasize that work on what has been spoiled will always have as its aim the creation of conditions in which life and culture will be enabled to thrive and develop further, conditions that will benefit not only the individual or the state, but all of humanity. Any work that leads only to blame, retribution, suffering, or self-glorification continues to obscure understanding and results only in further limitation.

6/1st   Difficult early conditions in life that prevent or distort the free development of a child's sense of self and of safety in the world may lead to the contraction of hope and trust. As adults, this defensive self-limitation may pre-empt disappointment or rejection, but it is likely to carry an unconscious weight of anger that, turned outwards and used as a weapon, may alienate exactly those people whose attention or respect one is hoping to attract. It requires honesty, courage, and determination to release these patterns of behaviour, as well as endurance. If we rise to this challenge every aspect of our being will be affected, heart and mind, body and spirit.

9/2nd The trials of life amount to a continual assault for some of us. The concept of surrender can be understood in two different ways, the only difference between the two being that in one surrender is voluntary, and in the other it is forced. In the latter case power 'wins'; in the former, gentleness has the final word. If we are faced with a situation in which profound hurt or damage has been inflicted, then, if we are to eventually free ourselves from the shackles of helplessness or hate, we will need to move our work on to a deeper level, one on which issues of forgiveness and transformation can be contemplated.

9/3rd Circumstances may have taught us to mistrust our impulses and to tighten up if we feel we are in danger of losing control. Life without spontaneity is joyless, hardly more than existence. If we are to learn a more healthy abandon we may need to confront issues of shame and self-image. Each time we manage to loosen the grip of the past, even if it is only briefly, we affirm our right and our intention to live life more fully.

6/4th When we feel most invisible, most lost, most hopeless, we can use our suffering to connect to all other beings who have felt or are feeling as we are. There is a Buddhist practice that teaches us to use the in-breath to take in the darkness and pain of all those who are suffering as we are, and to use the out-breath to breathe out light and compassion to all, including ourselves. In this way our personal hurt is transformed into the recognition of universal suffering and the wish that others may be healed. We are likely to experience growing peace and healing ourselves if we follow such a practice.

6/5th Frequently we are not as powerless as we feel ourselves to be. If we only take into consideration the forces impacting

on us from without we may feel ill-equipped to act decisively; but if we make an honest appraisal of our own
strengths and resources and consider the consequences of
not acting in accord with our beliefs or vision, we may find
the balance tips in our favour. It can be very liberating to
make such an inventory and to question the rationale we
have constructed for our continuing passivity.

9/top   Stillness can become paralysis if it is the result of an anxious
contraction. From the outside this may look like the calm of
the Sage, but from within it will feel more desperate. Whenever we become aware that our capacity for openness and
our willingness to share are blocked, we need to reflect on
what fear is controlling us and whether or not our concern
is realistic. Our own growth will be restricted to the extent
that we resist this reflective work. A particular issue that
limits many in middle age and beyond is their attitude
towards younger people. Envy can inhibit the growth of
generosity that is such an important expression of maturity.
Growing old wisely generally requires a greater and greater
willingness to let go and let others take over.

19. Lin / Approach

Primary Trigrams

above *K'un* / The Receptive, Earth
below *Tui* / The Joyous, Lake

Nuclear Trigrams

above *K'un* / The Receptive, Earth
below *Chên* / The Arousing, Thunder

In general, the bottom two lines of a hexagram are considered to lie within the earth; the middle two to occupy the space on the surface of the earth and the top two to represent the realm of heaven. Thus, the Chinese New Year only begins when the growth that has been occurring below ground becomes visible, as represented by the hexagram *T'ai* / Peace. The present hexagram represents the twelfth and final month of the old year, at which point there is no visible evidence of this new growth; yet it is undeniably under way.

This hexagram reminds us about times of gestation, when it may appear that little or nothing is happening and life seems to shrink down to nothing more than waiting. Such times require patience and perseverance, particularly when the growth – or the process of change – that is taking place is doing so out of sight and beyond our control. This is not a time to try to intervene or force events forward more rapidly, as much as we may wish to do so. The presence of *Chên*, representing the instinct towards action and movement, reflects this impulse. That something is approaching is not in question – we do not have to rush to meet it, nor should we allow doubt to undermine our capacity for waiting. All the elements are present; nothing needs to be added or taken away.

Beyond the requirement for patience and trust there are other attitudes that may help us to honour this period of waiting as a 'season' in its own right, one in which we can prepare for the moment when that for which we have been waiting arrives. It is a time for attentive observation of small changes that might give us an indication of how the situation is developing, enabling us to make adjustments so that the movement is not obstructed, staying at all times grounded in the present, gathering information, remaining quietly centred. We cannot know how the process will play itself out or the shape or significance of the outcome, and we should avoid guessing at it. Commonsense is a great tool to develop at such a time.

A different approach to this hexagram is through the imagery of the shoreline, the area where the lake meets the land. The boundaries of this space are quite fluid, and the plants and creatures that inhabit it are able to move between more or less watery and more or less earthy environments. It is a transitional area. Times of waiting, while processes beyond our control work themselves out, are similar to this space and may offer us an opportunity to experiment with something new, allowing our imagination to stretch its wings. This sort of play not only relieves stress and nourishes us, it also creates openings, loosening structures and granting images and energies the freedom to evolve, to become, and then dissolve, without being named or shaped or held on to.

The Changing Lines

9/1st   The best beginning is made with commitment and a degree of clarity about one's strengths and weaknesses; however, a balance needs to be struck between trust in the process, wherever it may lead us, and a realistic appraisal of both the challenges we are likely to face and the resources we have at hand. If we falter at the outset, it does not signal failure, but rather that we have not completely understood the true nature of our undertaking or of the energies involved.

9/2nd   A setback can be disheartening, especially if it occurs as we are getting started. It can take the wind out of our sails and cause us to question our abilities and projects. This is not necessarily a bad thing; as long as we possess a degree of equanimity and a sense of humour, we will be able to benefit from whatever learning comes from the situation. It may be that we are over-estimating the degree to which we must be active in making things happen; natural growth progresses without intervention; our job is to nurture the young growth and protect it from careless or anxious handling.

6/3rd   As we feel a 'quickening' within the situation – a sense that the growth that has been happening largely out of sight is now viable – a surge of energy may carry us into a new and experientially more dynamic phase. We should enjoy this blooming of promise fully; the recognition that it will not last forever need not spoil our appreciation of it at this moment.

6/4th   At a certain point many of us 'wake up' and find that we have barely been aware of living up to this moment, and now it seems that life is running out. We have allowed ourselves to be carried by the tides of expectation or opportunity (and this is perfectly natural and appropriate) and for the first time the next step seems unclear. This can be a frightening realization, but also an exciting one; our engagement with Life itself stands to be refreshed and deepened.

6/5th   If we lose touch with events that are happening at a distance and behave in a self-absorbed or exclusively self-referential manner, following our own agenda without thought for the consequences to others, we risk not only becoming isolated ourselves, but also increasing the burdens that others must bear. We are all connected in this web of life; there is no person and no action that lies outside it and its influence. Each of us bears a responsibility to all others and there is no true greatness that is not firmly rooted in this principle.

6/top   Blessings sometimes come from the least expected quarter and at the least expected moment. We can never predict, we can only remain as open as possible. The more complex our personal agenda is, the more exactly defined our idea of success, the less likely we are to be able to notice, leave alone to receive, such gifts.

20. Kuan / Contemplation (View)

Primary Trigrams

above *Sun* / The Gentle, Wind, Wood
below *K'un* / The Receptive, Earth

Nuclear Trigrams

above *Kên* / Keeping Still, Mountain
below *K'un* / The Receptive, Earth

This is a calendar hexagram representing the eighth month in the Chinese calendar, September–October, the month following the autumn equinox, when the light and dark lines were in balance but pulling apart (see Hexagram 12, *P'i* / Standstill). Now the dark lines are rising; the light are waning. Many, if not most, cultures observe festivals in which the light and the dark struggle with each other, the former finally vanquishing the latter. This is not a once-and-for-all victory, however: the struggle will be repeated as the cycle of seasons – or the myth-cycle of the culture – turns again to this particular theme. In Christian culture All Hallows Eve (Hallowe'en) and All Saints Day (31 October and 1 November) mark this point in the cycle. The dead return for one night – frightening, possibly vengeful, hungry, perhaps lonely – and the way we greet them is critical. We must 'treat' them well, welcome them, feed them, maybe recognize our own loved ones under the skeleton's or witch's or ghost's masks or forms, but then we send them on their way again. Respecting the dead, the dark, the forces of destruction, fearing them appropriately but acknowledging them and their belonging-ness in the wider scheme of life is wise. If not treated well, they 'trick' us. They creep up on us when we are not looking and can wreak havoc. This is as true within an individual as it is in a culture. The dark is always with us; suffering, cruelty, loss, envy, hatred, ignorance, fear. When these forces are denied;

when we fail to struggle with them and, instead, arrogate them to 'others', when we allow ourselves to forget that it is the cyclical engagement between light and dark that keeps the balance healthy, then we set the stage for them to explode dangerously on to the scene.

Having considered the seasonal associations of this hexagram, it is appropriate to look at it from a different and more general perspective. The construction of the hexagram resembles a high platform or vantage point, a position from which one may gain a wide perspective while also becoming visible oneself. Such a position is generally reserved for important events or powerful individuals. Humanity, symbolized by *K'un*, is placed at the base of the platform, like an audience. The rudimentary elements of a 'theatre' are thus represented. When we enter a theatrical space we have some expectation of transformation; things will not be exactly as they seem to be. We hope to be not just entertained, but changed in some way, and entering this space is therefore a choice based on hope, even faith. We look to the actors to do more than just act; we hope they will themselves be transformed for the period of the play and thus testify to a greater truth than that we have left behind when we entered. We hope for an experience of renewal.

Such hopes are characteristic of our approach to any individual for whom we have particular respect, to whom we 'look up'. We want to believe in wisdom, in vision, in the possibility of transformation, and there are individuals who seem to have grasped or embody a different view of human events, a different understanding of life and death. The individual who has vision, who has studied the nature and meaning of life and death, looking deeply into herself as well as into all that passes before her, who meditates and reflects on what she sees, will herself have a profound effect on others and her influence will be greater than she can imagine. Those we regard as wise seem to have a great capacity for receptivity; they seem to be genuinely interested in whatever appears before them, granting it attention and respect; they have a still presence that affects all those with whom they have contact; their views are sought because they are without personal ambition.

A further consideration arising from the structure of the hexagram is the value of gaining a wider perspective. Seeing events *sub specie aeternitatis* means putting things in perspective, adjusting our viewpoint from the focused, immediate, and personal to a more expanded and inclusive view. More often than not our moods and choices are shaped by impulse and habit, by a narrow, well-rehearsed narrative of who we are, what we do, how the world is. If we can remove ourselves even briefly from the pressures of day-to-day conflicts, we are often able to gain a different perspective on issues large and small. This hexagram reminds us of that fact.

The Changing Lines

6/1st   Acknowledging need or ignorance may be an important first step in gaining new perspectives. If we have framed our path in terms of challenges and heroic deeds, then we have set ourselves on a solitary way and we may find it difficult to accept offers of advice or assistance from those who have something to share. By opening ourselves to guidance from whatever direction it might appear, we make room for the unexpected.

6/2nd The 'vision quest' is an ancient rite of passage that challenges the initiate to endure hardship in search of a personal vision. If we are seeking enlightenment, we are undertaking a vision quest, and we will, sooner or later, have to confront our greatest fears, our 'demons'. Once they have entered our awareness and been acknowledged, they are likely to loosen their grip and may, eventually, serve as a valuable foundation for our personal vision and growth.

6/3rd Sometimes it feels as if we will lose out if we do not keep moving, that if we take time out everything we have achieved will fall away. This is rarely true. Putting down deep roots allows a tree to grow in the most difficult and testing environments, and the same can be said of human beings. Guidance begins to come from within, not in the limited terms of ego, but in terms of seeing more clearly the long-term effects of our choices on both our own life and the lives of others.

6/4th Even when we have achieved a good deal, become more self-aware, reflective, and serious, we may continue to feel unfulfilled or dissatisfied if we have not fully experienced challenge and risk and possibly disapproval and criticism. For better or worse, we may need to step out of our relative obscurity, taking the risk that the choice to become more visible will result in difficulties that cannot be envisioned. We may even feel regret when it does not work out as we had hoped; none the less, we have taken the first step towards living more creatively, more in the moment, and others will follow.

9/5th   Learning how to 'travel light' is the best preparation for the final release required by death, but it is also of great benefit throughout life. It means not having an agenda that we carry around with us, being content to assume a degree of power or responsibility, but also being happy to relinquish it. Trusting the wisdom of Life itself enables us to live fully in the present while accepting that all things end. It allows us to open to experiences of every sort without being crippled by fear of 'failure' or of making a 'mistake'.

9/top   'All rivers lead to the sea.' In the final analysis, our achievements do not live and die with us any more than do our choices affect only ourselves. Rather, they join and swell the river of experience that flows from other times, other cultures, other individuals. Whatever we create, for good or for ill, becomes a living inheritance for those who follow.

21. Shih Ho / Biting Through

Primary Trigrams

above *Li* / The Clinging, Fire
below *Chên* / The Arousing, Thunder

Nuclear Trigrams

above *K'an* / The Abysmal, Water
below *Kên* / Keeping Still, Mountain

The firm line in the fourth position of this hexagram represents an obstacle that is preventing the jaws from closing. (This image is directly related to hexagram *27: I / Corners of the Mouth.*) This position is often the most difficult of the six to interpret: it lies in the middle of the hexagram, or situation, and is considered to be naturally yielding, yet its very unobtrusiveness means that it can act without drawing attention to itself. While it is past the crucial third or middle position, it nevertheless constitutes part of both nuclear trigrams as well as the upper primary trigram, thus participating in the action as a whole as well as its denouement. It follows that the obstruction in question may be neither obvious nor easy to tease out, and its appearance may belie its influence.

Whatever the nature of the obstacle, the remedy, within the terms of this hexagram, is to be found in dealing with it, biting through it, not avoiding it or waiting for it to disappear. *Chên* has a strong, naturally ascending motion indicating vigorous action and determination. *Li* indicates clarity of judgement and openness or lack of prejudice. Also, as Fire, *Li* has the capacity to both consume and to test. *K'an* suggests there may be an element of danger inherent in the conditions of the time; however, as water (also *K'an*) finds its way around or over obstacles and always remains true to itself, so a combination of unwavering commitment to deal with the obstruction and sincerity of heart in the manner chosen is the way forward. Finally, *Kên* refers to a capacity for thoughtfulness and insight. All of these qualities notwithstanding, if something must be bitten through, it is certain that the best way to do it is to get on with it. Too gentle a bite will not suffice; too violent a bite might end up damaging one's own teeth or jaws.

In the *Appended Judgements* that accompany this hexagram in Book III of Wilhelm's *I Ching* (1989, p. 490), the images of the sun (*Li*) and activity (*Chên*) are associated with the marketplace. Wherever human beings congregate and enjoy freedom of expression there will be those who seek to spread division and mistrust, to limit the exchange of ideas and to discourage independent creativity. This is a form of obstruction that we must not tolerate. It may be that taking a small but decisive stand as soon as a potentially compromising situation is recognized will clear the air with no further difficulties being encountered; however, waiting and hoping is an inadequate response that only encourages the consolidation or accumulation of obstacles. Wisdom resides in dealing with blockages when we first become aware of them, before they become big problems. In that way they will not become big problems.

A further, if tangential, consideration is the possibility that the obstruction might have a positive function, to slow one down, to prevent the too-hasty resolution of an uncomfortable situation. At times closure may be premature and signal avoidance of disharmony rather than a true coming together.

The Changing Lines

9/1st   When we are strongly motivated to get past an obstacle or through a difficult time and are not prepared to postpone this effort, our very decisiveness – perhaps, courage – will have an effect on resolving the situation and further confrontation may not be necessary. It is true to say that the more decisively we deal with a potentially troublesome situation as soon as it appears, the more we reduce the chances that it will ever develop into a 'problem'. Many of our heaviest burdens exist because we have avoided addressing them immediately. Once we have done so, we experience such great relief that it is surprising we do not learn to always take on small hurdles before they become big ones.

6/2nd In general, if we are not party to a particular disagreement or difficulty, we do well to stay out of it and not exacerbate the situation or draw the fire to ourselves. However, at times we cannot remain aside from events and our contribution, even if it seems to make matters worse, may serve to reveal conflicts that were previously hidden and lead to greater clarity for all. This should not be used as a justification for behaving impulsively or carelessly.

6/3rd In some situations we find ourselves needing to consider whether it is best not to pre-empt events but rather be moved by them, or to act independently, proactively. If we are strongly affected by what is happening, it may be that we will opt for action on the basis that at least something will be clarified if we resist the paralysis that can be the effect of conflict and step out into the light.

9/4th In terms of the structure of the hexagram, this is where the obstruction lies. The situation has already developed to a considerable extent; that is, the obstruction is not to be encountered in the early stages, but, rather, in circumstances where we might have thought the way forward to be relatively clear. In fact, at such a moment we might be tempted to relax and take our eye 'off the ball'. Now we may need to address ourselves to personal or 'inner' work in order to gain insight into how – or if – we are creating or contributing to the blockage.

6/5th Sometimes a degree of detachment (that some might label 'ruthlessness', in an attempt to discourage us) is necessary in order to handle an awkward situation resolutely and unambiguously. If our nature is such that we find it difficult to view others and their behaviour critically, then we will find such times trying. If we need, in fact, to view our own behaviour with a more critical eye, then this could present us with a real challenge. If we can rise to the challenge our sense of freedom, personal strength, and capacity for creative living may be greatly enhanced.

9/top We may be called upon to simply stay in place while others take the difficult decisions that resolve a conflict. In this case our support should be unambiguous, even if we effectively 'do' nothing. It is rarely difficult to give the appearance of being present while actually distancing ourselves from what is taking place, but we should not permit ourselves to follow this inclination. Once the time of resolute action is past we should step aside and allow events to proceed, content in the knowledge that our contribution was whole-hearted and we have nothing to regret.

22. Pi / Grace

Primary Trigrams

above *Kên* / Keeping Still, Mountain
below *Li* / The Clinging, Fire

Nuclear Trigrams

above *Chên* / The Arousing, Thunder
below *K'an* / The Abysmal, Water

The light within the mountain; clarity clinging to stillness. In the context of this hexagram, Grace has a number of meanings; one is that of a gift from God, from the Universe, given freely, something that cannot be earned or won. Another is being in an entirely natural state, like fire, pure and unadorned. A further meaning arises out of the lovely image of radiance within the stillness of the mountain that leads to considerations about beauty of form, something that may be appreciated but is not necessarily to be trusted. Finally, in that this image is so very still and essentially non-physical, an image of pure contemplation, almost disembodied, the subject of detachment from ordinary physical life in the pursuit of enlightenment is considered.

For some it seems that living life as a spiritual path means distancing oneself from material existence, while for others it means being in touch – as an artist is – with the inner beauty that illuminates the 'object'. There is a story about two monks who sat gazing at and contemplating a particular tree for hours. Finally, one turned to the other and said, 'They call that a tree'. The two monks laughed heartily. The monks were contemplating the form before them, but they were not seeing a child's picture-book 'Tree'; they were (we can imagine) deeply connected to an inner light and life, an inner reality and radiance far transcending the apparently solid and familiar object that we call a tree. In touch with this vastness, they found the name we have chosen and use so confidently most amusing. In other words, the contemplative moment or life may lead to either a deeper connection with all life or a wilful detachment from it. We must return to the world ultimately and take and live – or bear witness to – our insights there.

Each of the trigrams that constitute *Pi* is associated with a major heavenly body – the sun and moon, the Great Bear (or Big Dipper), and the familiar constellations. By noting, questioning, and learning to calculate the movements of these bodies, we are able to determine the time of day and the season as well as estimate our latitude; we can 'position' ourselves. This reflects one of the great themes of the *I Ching*, that through observing the nature and qualities of all that moves in heaven and all that lives on earth we can come to understand our own nature and act in harmony with ourselves and within the cosmos. This is not a simple recipe for a pallid alignment with nature, but, rather, a powerful directive for a penetrating and mindful consideration of the forms that surround and shape our lives – whether on a macrocosmic or microcosmic stage – and of how we choose to position ourselves in relation to them.

The relationship between form and content is an intriguing one that relates to the age-old questions of what sort of creatures we are and what sort of a creation we inhabit. In general, yin lines are considered formless; yang lines give them form by limiting them. Yet *K'un*, which consists only of yielding lines, represents the earth, that most solid of objects, and is, in addition, considered to take into herself the formless 'seed' of *Ch'ien*, Heaven, and, through a process of gestation, to give birth to all things. Perhaps all we can say is that the content of everything is the Tao; the forms are merely transient, ephemeral manifestations of that undivided unity. The weight that we give them is of our choosing rather than intrinsic to their nature. These reflections may indicate that a possible – and radical – 'message' of this hexagram is that we need to open our minds to the mystery and radiance of the universe and ourselves within it at this time, to loosen up the ties of what we think we know or have named, and to create a space that may be filled by a new and unexpected understanding.

The Changing Lines

A natural movement upwards through the hexagram (or movement through a particular situation or period of time), is assumed;

whether we co-operate with this process or resist it will depend on who we are and what we want. The commentary on any given line will always start with this assumption of motion or evolution and then evaluate the type of behaviour that is most appropriate for the individual, given the characteristics of line and position (yielding or firm). In this hexagram, the focus is on the shift of emphasis that happens as we mature from a concentration on form to one on content.

9/1st   A strong line in a strong position, but, given the emphasis on emptiness and lack of conceit, this early drive may represent uneasiness with not-knowing or over-attachment to form. Unfocused personal ambition becomes frustrated quickly and works against the slow growth of understanding and quiet centredness that this hexagram explores.

6/2nd   This yielding line represents the open heart of the fire; in terms of the hexagram, it provides the entry point for grace. The relationship between emptiness and radiance falls into the category of mystery, in that we can neither analyse nor create it. Its force and effect are beyond question, while its nature is unhurried, attentive, and easy.

9/3rd   The question of who we really are is one that preoccupies most of us at some point in life. Generally, we define ourselves by our roles and occupations, what we 'do', but what we 'are' is revealed only indirectly or glimpsed fleetingly. The way in which we think of ourselves lies somewhere between appearance and intuition. How we treat ourselves – thoughtfully, carelessly, contemptuously – will reflect all these levels of self-experience. By choosing to treat ourselves differently we can begin to learn more about our innermost being.

6/4th   The first half of life is often concerned with establishing oneself in the world, consolidating a sense of self built on relationships and achievements. The workings of grace and the growth of our inner 'light' do not concern us much. However, a time comes for many of us when we do begin to wonder what it is all about, what we are all about, whether we want to continue more or less as things are, or whether there is 'more'. We may seek some sort of enlightenment, and a new part of the journey begins, with more awareness and concentration. 'Youth shows but half; trust God, see all, nor be afraid' (Browning, 1956, 'Rabbi Ben Ezra').

6/5th   The fifth position often reflects a degree of visibility or responsibility. Even when we are mature ourselves, we often have unrealistic expectations of those who hold office or have leadership roles. It is as if we allow parts of ourselves never to grow up. Those who bear themselves with grace rarely consider it helpful to blame or judge others. They recognize that what we have in common vastly outweighs that which divides us.

9/top   The dialectic between form and content that has been the subject of this hexagram reaches a new level here as we reach the firm line that has contained and shaped elemental fire. As the top line of *Kên*, Mountain, it represents the Sage whose exemplary life is led with absolute simplicity; form and content have become indivisible. For those of us who have yet to attain such grace-full-ness, the subject of our personal 'light' – how we discover it, cultivate it, nourish it, use it – will be a continuing focus for reflection.

23. Po / Splitting Apart (Letting Go / Release)

Primary Trigrams

above *Kên* / Keeping Still, Mountain
below *K'un* / The Receptive, Earth

Nuclear Trigrams

above *K'un* / The Receptive, Earth
below *K'un* / The Receptive, Earth

This is a calendar hexagram representing the ninth month in the Chinese calendar, October–November, the turning point from autumn to winter. The next month (November–December) is represented by the hexagram *K'un* / The Receptive, all earth, all winter, no light. The remaining firm or 'light' line at the top of the present hexagram is seen as the seed or fruit that must be released at this time and allowed to fall into the earth, where it can germinate. This moment is very important: to be able to let go of the last bit of light and entrust it to the dark, receptive earth, not knowing when or if it will come to life again, requires trust in deep invisible processes. Letting go at the appropriate moment can be difficult, particularly if we cannot see where our next handhold will be. Our inclination may well be to work against the time, to reach back to the season of fullness that we have recently enjoyed. But the movement towards dark and winter is also towards gestation and new birth – life renewing itself – and we need to trust this process wholeheartedly.

The movement of *K'un*, Earth, repeated three times in this hexagram, in the primary and nuclear trigrams, is downward, and so *Kên*, Mountain is, quite literally, undermined by the natural sinking movement of the earth. A steep and high mountain will erode more quickly than a low, rounded one. So too, we are more likely to experience times such as that pictured in this hexagram, if we have isolated ourselves in a sort of 'ivory tower'. The ground beneath our feet can be taken away more easily when we are only in touch with a very small patch of earth, with all that represents in terms of humanity and human fellowship.

The theme of splitting apart, the imagery of erosion and under-mining, reflect the difficult energies of this time. As in the myth of Sisyphus, where he is condemned to an eternity of pushing a boul-der uphill only to have it roll back down again, this may be a time when nothing 'works', and the boulder always ends up where it started. To recognize such a time for what it is, and to call a halt to trying to reverse it or struggle against it, is the beginning of wisdom; the process needs to be allowed to work through its own cycle, to purge itself.

Not only the seed falls in the autumn, so also do the leaves of a tree, and where they fall, they decay and are returned to the soil. This is our human fate as well – natural but also inconceivable – and reminders of our mortality may be more apparent or insistent at this time. Yet we are never helpless; there is always a natural movement to the times that, if we can align ourselves with it, will carry us through present difficulties on its own wave of energy. Here, the alignment needs to be with the earth, with other beings, with our inherent generosity, and with the tide of the seasons. We need to join all the other creatures with whom we share this earth, reconnect to our own 'creatureliness'. In so doing we may find the warmth and companionship that are the rewards of this time.

The Changing Lines

An alternative approach to the lines is through the language and imagery of the chakras, the different energy centres of the body, the loci of our identity. As we mature and develop these temporary identifications shift and build upon each other. Earlier identifica-tions will be superseded by later ones, but never eliminated. In time, each self-definition must be released in order for an expansion of awareness and experience to take place and be integrated. The first line is the base chakra, which represents our root, our home; the second is the sacral, representing the instinctual urge to form rela-tionships and move into an intimate connection with the world; the third lies in the solar plexus and represents our relationship with ourself, our individuality; the fourth is the heart chakra; the fifth the throat *chakra*, the voice; the sixth the third eye, our intuition. As we mature, our identity moves from the first through to the sixth, embracing, finally, our deepest source of knowing, our intuition. There is a seventh *chakra* that lies above the head, the crown *chakra*, associated with the spirit.

6/1st   Letting go of the security afforded by the 'light', the known, is never easy. The sooner we recognize that we are facing this loss, the sooner we can begin to prepare ourselves for it by looking at our priorities, reflecting on our fears, seeking help if we feel we need it. This is relating to oneself and the situation in a very thoughtful and congruent way, with a readiness to make appropriate decisions and act on them. It is the opposite of denial.

6/2nd   Whereas a child delights in the unknown and experiences everything in a fresh and inquisitive manner, as adults we do all we can to eliminate the unknown and seem to yearn for relationships to things and to people that require no thought and are not unsettled by change. If we would regain that freshness, we have only to loosen the grip of our mind; the world is made afresh before our eyes, every moment absolutely new and unique.

6/3rd   If we are able to align ourselves with the deep processes and energies of the earth – the Tao – we will find that whatever happens we are able to release our resistance to it and allow its reality to bear us. This connectedness to what *is*, rather than what we would have *be*, affords profound relief; the next step is clearer if we see where we are standing now.

6/4th   The difference between passive and active acceptance is an important one. The latter creates clarity and a sense of participation in the process, while the former is more akin to shutting down, shutting off, giving up. Further, in relation to the times pictured here, it is likely that the former would view these conditions as a defeat while the latter would view them as simply a manifestation of the natural cycles of life of which we are a part; there is no 'victim' here. Our point of view makes all the difference.

6/5th   A yielding line in this important position reflects the wisdom of consenting to the imminent loss or change pictured here. We can go a step further and consider visibly aligning ourselves with the agent or process of change. Becoming visible means taking a stand, acting responsibly when we know others might be looking for a lead from us, or even when we are the only ones who will see and appreciate our choice. It might mean speaking out. The change addressed by this hexagram may be taking place unopposed, when questions should be being asked or the process should be subject to more reflection.

9/top The seed that drops to the earth and is taken into the soil to become a new plant is an example of the endless process of making and unmaking and re-making that *is* our universe. In a sense, we have all been present since the universe began, as no new mass or energy has been or ever will be created. Our fears about loss of control and the unknown may be put into perspective if we truly appreciate how awesome is the fact of life itself, how improbable is our own existence.

24. Fu / Return (The Turning Point)

Primary Trigrams

above *K'un* / The Receptive, Earth
below *Chên* / The Arousing, Thunder

Nuclear Trigrams

above *K'un* / The Receptive, Earth
below *K'un* / The Receptive, Earth

All change, as reflected in the *I Ching*, takes place in six stages as a line moves from the lowest position to the top of the hexagram, and when it leaves from the top it returns as the bottom line. The famous passage in Ecclesiastes is entirely relevant: 'To everything there is a season and a time for every purpose under heaven . . .'. The seasons move between the two solstices from the heights and fruitfulness of summer to the depths and apparent barrenness of winter, and our lives also move between the poles of fullness and emptiness, one giving way gradually to the other, both essential and natural; the seed must ripen and then fall, and the earth must lie fallow in order to receive and regenerate the seed. This hexagram represents the moment when the seed quickens, although it is still underground and will take time to mature. It is the eleventh month of the Chinese calendar (December–January)and the winter solstice has just taken place. This moment represents an extraordinarily important turning point in the year when the long descent into darkness ceases and, out of sight, the ascent towards the light begins again. Before calendars as we know them were invented, monuments that marked this moment, this rebirth, were constructed around the world. These primitive calendars provided a threshold over which the first light of the new season would fall and be witnessed and celebrated.

New births are always a cause for joy, but what is newborn is also vulnerable and tender, and must be treated appropriately and with care. The new growth is represented by the forceful *Chên*, the sign in which 'God comes forth . . .' to 'seed' the world. It is a time of promise and renewal and it is vitally important that we should recognize this new beginning, and also acknowledge the reality of an ending. Doubt is the enemy of this moment, and of whatever purpose informs this moment.

T. S. Eliot, in his remarkable meditation on time in the *Four Quartets*, writes, 'What we call the beginning is often the end / And to make an end is to make a beginning'. Within the context of the present hexagram, this paradox is explored: new life is symbolized by the entry of the single yang line, but that is not all, because return can also be understood as that moment when we turn back towards the beginning, perhaps for a new beginning, perhaps to see again where we began.

The Changing Lines

There is a further interpretation to consider when we look at the changing lines, and that is 'Return' as the moment when, for whatever reason, the individual turns around, choosing not to pursue her present course of action or thought. According to this interpretation, as the distance from the first line increases it becomes more difficult to turn back, to reconsider the choice that was made, and this accords with general experience. While the following comments do not enlarge on this understanding, it is something that may be taken into consideration in meditating on the significance of any particular line change.

9/1st   This strong line in the first position represents the 'seed', still in the earth but ready to sprout. It also represents a positive and energetic response to the chance of a new beginning, a new adventure. This response is only one of a number of possibilities, ranging from the very positive to the very negative. Whatever our response to this first sign of new life, whether we turn towards it or away from it, we can gain some understanding of ourselves by being as self-aware as possible.

6/2nd   The seed has become a seedling, but it may still show little sign of its future shape or strength. We sometimes expect too much too soon, and either force premature growth or become disappointed and turn to something more dynamic. New growth needs support, protection, and, above all, patience.

6/3rd This line represents the turning point within the hexagram, lying, as it does, between coming and going, inner and outer, before and after. When we find ourselves in this position, we should seek to understand the underlying dynamics and to clarify our own views before we take any decision; otherwise, we may run the risk of becoming entangled in complex currents.

6/4th When the source of movement is at some distance from us there may be no need for us to acknowledge or respond to it. When the time comes for us to do so, we may be taken unawares. The best preparation for this moment is to develop an authentic sense of personal values that are both open and non-negotiable. This combination enables us to stay grounded and centred when new challenges confront us.

6/5th At any point in life the decision to make a new start is one that is likely to be tested early and often. These tests challenge and strengthen our heart energies and keep us on the path. We become warriors through such trials and develop stillness as well as courage.

6/top It is never too late to wake up and start learning. It may only be when we see the end of a situation approaching that we are sufficiently relieved or regretful that we take notice of that which is passing; we may have been unaware of it until this moment. In this way, endings can be great teachers if we take the opportunity to review and reflect on where we have been and the choices we have made.

25. Wu Wang / Innocence (The Unexpected)

Primary Trigrams

above *Ch'ien* / The Creative, Heaven
below *Chên* / The Arousing, Thunder

Nuclear Trigrams

above *Sun* / The Penetrating, Wind, Wood
below *Kên* / Keeping Still, Mountain

The meaning of 'innocent' derives from the Latin, *nocere*, to hurt or harm. Innocence is not-harming, harmlessness. It is important to differentiate unconscious innocence, a condition of the very young and the hapless, from a more consciously cultivated attitude of trusting mindfulness and lack of prejudice. If it is rigorous and not simply disingenuous (open-eyed rather than wide-eyed), then this attitude leads to a quiet readiness to welcome whatever appears, a lack of fearfulness, spaciousness, and the absence of self-seeking behaviour.

At any point in life, but particularly in the early stages of a new project, we may be inclined towards high ideals and choices based on the most elevated of principles. There is an innocence in this attitude that may enable us to stride forth into even the most threatening of situations where, if we were to be more calculating, we would hold back. As long it sustains us, there is no harm in it, but as soon as we have to sustain the attitude in order to keep going, innocence – especially if it is accompanied by impulsiveness – will prove itself to be insufficiently robust to withstand even the ordinary trials of life. Where it is strong enough to meet and even welcome challenges without sacrificing the original spaciousness and absence of personal agenda, innocence will have been tempered into something like wisdom.

This hexagram consists of two primary trigrams indicating energetic movement forwards and upwards. The trigram of Heaven draws the trigram of Thunder and of beginnings towards it; in a sense, it gives it its blessing. The balancing principles that reflect the more human experience of life and its challenges are indicated by the attributes of the two nuclear trigrams: a gathered and quiet attitude (*Kên*, Keeping Still, Mountain) that is not rushed into action or reaction, and a capacity for endurance and perseverance in working towards a chosen goal (the attributes of *Sun*, Wind, Wood). When the unexpected occurs we can bend to its effect and not break if we can maintain stillness, resilience, and our connection to the Tao. A demonstration of this can be seen in the winter, when we might notice a branch carrying more and more snow until, with a gentle movement, it bends a bit more and the snow slides off. This is, perhaps, the key: the success of innocence lies in a natural flexibility, in the absence of artifice or deceit, in the lack of attachment to any particular outcome, in a willingness to entrust oneself to the 'will of Heaven', the unknown, the mystery, the Tao. The more we can give up our need to know and to control and align ourselves and our plans with the energies, the 'flow' of the moment, the less will we be encumbered by fears and destabilized by apparent obstacles, trusting that wherever the road ends up will be all right. There is great power in this attitude because, as in the hexagram, all our energy will be moving in the same direction without the 'drag' of anxieties about how it will all turn out. In brief, innocence must be hard won or it will be simply – and dangerously – naïve.

The Changing Lines

9/1st   The innocent attitude described above should not be confused with passivity. The energy of life strains for expression and experience or it falters and dies. Hesitation or doubt create a poor basis for starting out and can undermine courage and commitment. There is a Jewish proverb, 'Over every blade of grass an angel hovers, whispering, 'Grow, grow'. The angel can encourage, but it cannot force growth. We must do our part.

6/2nd   The young are fearless and eager. The drive to learn and gather skills comes from within, but it is shaped by watching and copying others, even by challenging them, long before the necessary strength has been developed to make a serious challenge. We tolerate the chaos and demands that attend human growth because we enjoy its energy and recognize its necessity. There are lessons here for growth at all stages of life.

6/3rd   Over time we learn how open or candid we can afford to be in different settings or with different people. At times we may feel our trust has been betrayed, and that can be a useful piece of learning if we stay open and curious about how it happened rather than closing down or becoming cynical. Innocence, at its best, implies a willingness to start again, without an agenda, to engage with others without prejudice, to see ourselves and others clearly but without judgement, to treat life as an adventure without expecting it always to have a happy ending.

9/4th   Everywhere there are unobtrusive people who quietly go about the business of living life in a kind, generous, and thoughtful manner. Most are unaware that they are doing anything unusual, leave alone exceptional; they act in this way without thinking about it and with no 'audience' in mind. There are far more of these people than we might imagine, and it can be good to remind ourselves from time to time that this world, which can appear so cynical and exploitative, contains a great deal of uncomplicated human warmth and care.

9/5th   Cultivating an unprejudiced and open attitude does not excuse us from responsibility when firm action must be taken. In fact, the more we give the impression of being 'soft', the more likely it is that we will be tested. When innocence is not contrived or shallow; when it reflects its original meaning of not doing harm; when it conveys clarity and honesty, then it is highly respected. But it must win that respect and not turn away from challenge and complexity.

9/top   There is no limit to the way of innocence when it is understood on a deep level. Although circumstances change and new situations require new choices, if we approach each day and each person essentially empty of prejudgement and open to communication, we will be prepared for anything and more ready to delight in the unexpected, the fleeting. As always, when describing this quality, it sounds easy and even inconsequential; it is anything but.

26. Ta Chu / The Taming Power of the Great

Primary Trigrams

above Kên / Keeping Still, Mountain
below Ch'ien / The Creative, Heaven

Nuclear Trigrams

above Chên / The Arousing, Thunder
below Tui / The Joyous, Lake

The forms and energies of Life are infinite in their variety. For better or worse, consciously or unconsciously, we are active participants in the work of creation: every action, every choice we make, our words and thoughts have an effect, bringing something new into the world that then has a life of its own. This is how 'karma' works. The 'Greatness' referred to in this hexagram is the power of stillness, of stopping, of awareness, and, further, the accumulated wisdom and guidance that we find in great teachers and thinkers, in literature and the arts. The creative force of Life works through us, but we shape it, give it form and direction. The greater our awareness of ourselves as creators, the greater must be our sense of responsibility towards what we choose to release into the world. The 'Great' among us tend to say little, to use their influence or power infrequently but courageously. They have 'tamed' the tremendous potential and force of the personal ego through hardship or self-discipline, and they are, therefore, able to 'tame', to contain and channel, the immense, primal, undivided, and amoral force of Creativity.

To tame is not to break, nor is it to appropriate; it is to gentle and to harness the strength of something wild and natural. It implies a relationship and a responsibility. This is a balance of great delicacy that can only be effective if it is open and transparent, based on integrity and nurtured by continuing awareness practice. The misuse or abuse of trust is a form of betrayal.

The emphasis at this time should be on self-awareness. When the Creative is seeking expression, pressing to be given form, we must be thoroughly grounded and able to wait and reflect on the degree to which our own self-aggrandizement is at the core of the urge to act. Spending time with others, sharing some of our ideas or visions with those we trust and respect, allowing some space and air to penetrate the moment, can help us to clarify our choices before we make important decisions.

The Changing Lines

9/1st   There are times when we feel almost paralysed, unable to make choices, to exercise our creativity, or simply to move on and take advantage of opportunities that present themselves. The key to freeing ourselves does not lie in finding an external cause for our discomfort but rather in seeking to understand how unresolved issues may be holding us back, how we may, on some level, be confusing the dynamics of our present circumstances with similar ones in the past.

9/2nd   While containing our energy rather than wasting it is the general counsel, we need to be wary lest containment becomes an end in itself. Our long-term aim is to grow in wisdom and generosity through aligning ourselves with the Tao, and it is to this end that we hold back at this time, not to enhance our self-image. We should reflect on our motivation before we choose, if possible, but it is never too late to take an honest look at what we hope to achieve and why.

9/3rd   At times, the way forward starts with a step backwards. Another way of illustrating this principle is to consider the age-old ritual of sacrificing something before setting off on an important journey or quest. The alchemists prefaced their work with the prayer, 'Deo concedente', 'God willing'. Simply put, there is a form of yielding that acknowledges that the outcome of our endeavours cannot be known and therefore we make some gesture towards the Unknown that signifies our willingness to be diminished on a material level in order to gain wisdom or benefit on a spiritual level.

6/4th   The energy of life and creativity would seem to be unstoppable; however, if we impose a schedule or regime on ourselves that leaves no space for experiment and self-expression, and therefore devalues those activities, we might end by having little or no connection with our own imagination. On the other hand, if we value the imagination and encourage ourselves and others to play and try out different ways of being, without fearing the chaos that may well precede the creation, we align ourselves with all that is lively and brilliant in the world.

6/5th   This yielding line in the important fifth position reflects the central message of this hexagram, that a sort of transformation may occur if we can accept restraint or learn to hold back and contain our drives and appetites, not attempting to squash or divert them, simply acknowledging and embracing them without acting on them. An extraordinary strength and clarity can develop from this practice.

9/top   The top position represents the concluding moments of the situation pictured in the hexagram. This firm line representing the mountain has acted as the central agent shaping the requirements of the time. As important as recognizing the necessity for holding back may be, it is equally as important to recognize when that necessity no longer exists, when we can relax and enjoy a new 'season'.

27. I / Corners of the Mouth (Providing Nourishment)

Primary Trigrams

above *Kên* / Keeping Still, Mountain
below *Chên* / The Arousing, Thunder

Nuclear Trigrams

above *K'un* / The Receptive, Earth
below *K'un* / The Receptive, Earth

The name of the hexagram, taken from the firm and yielding lines that resemble an open mouth, suggests that we are considering a very ordinary, human feature and its activities, eating and speaking, taking in and giving out. The bracketed title – 'Providing Nourishment' – points in a somewhat different direction, or indicates the manner in which we are to reflect on this image. Provision involves thinking ahead, being actively aware of what is necessary, choosing consciously. And nourishing is more than just feeding; it suggests the aim of supporting growth and health. Observation of how and with what we nourish ourselves can tell us a good deal about what we value. Similarly, the words that we speak may come out thoughtlessly, with little awareness of their potential to harm or to nurture, or they may be chosen with care. The things we tell ourselves, the thoughts and stories with which we feed ourselves, can also be chosen with care or allowed free rein to unsettle, provoke, or shape our moods.

The structure of the hexagram emphasizes the importance of these considerations. *Chên* represents the beginning of all things, the first time that the seed of Heaven fertilizes Earth, creating a new being. In the passage from the *Shuo Kua* / Discussion of the Trigrams quoted in Appendix A, we find, 'God comes forth in the sign of the Arousing', that is, *Chên*. The final sign of the sequence is *Kên*, Mountain, representing the place where all things pass away.

Again, the relevant passage from the *Shuo Kua* reads, 'He brings all things to perfection in the sign of Keeping Still'; that is, *Kên*. This hexagram, therefore, represents the beginning of all motion and the ending, or perfecting, of it. As our words leave our mouths they take on a life of their own; they may give rise to actions for which we will bear some responsibility, for we have nourished the growth of something in speaking.

Finally, the open lines in the middle of this hexagram represent Earth, that upon which we are all ultimately dependent for our nourishment. We could also consider them to represent 'common' sense that is not at all the same thing as unconsciousness but is, rather, an earthed and realistic capacity to judge the requirements of the moment and to not go beyond the moment.

The Changing Lines

9/1st   Hunger is a primitive drive. Whatever it is hunger for (food, love, meaning), without it the will to live simply drains away. Under life-threatening conditions people must simply endure and wait: for a new treatment, for rain, for next year's harvest, for change. If we find ourselves waiting and enduring without good reason, we should ask ourselves where our hunger has gone, what we are waiting for and why.

6/2nd   Most religions incorporate the practice of fasting for those seeking enlightenment. Much can be gained from discovering that we can do with less, that simplification can lead to enrichment and empowerment. The practice encourages us to confront our fears and to develop a more profound trust of ourselves and of what lies beyond our grasp.

6/3rd   Throughout life we must continually reassess our priorities; in particular, the balance between attention to form and appearance, on the one hand, and to content of mind and heart on the other. Midway through life is often a time when we are more or less forced to reconsider this balance, and the greater our self-awareness is the more rewarding will this process be. It begins and ends with the question: how do I nourish myself and what aspect of myself do I prioritize?

6/4th   The reasons why we might choose to reject nourishment or health, in the widest sense, are often to do with either resentment or fear. Taking responsibility for ourselves, rather than blaming others, can feel more 'grown-up' than we wish to be, and more lonely. Anything that reminds us of our age reminds us of our mortality.

6/5th   Recognizing when we have enough, and passing that which is surplus to our own requirements on to others, is a sign of wisdom and trust. When others benefit from our willingness to share the goodness that we enjoy, an exchange and an expansion takes place that nourishes all of us.

9/top   When, on account of our experience or our particular gifts, we are needed to serve as a source of nourishment for others, we should attempt to respond to this need in a gentle and restrained manner, not with a show of self-importance or in the expectation of reward. When the time for such care or attention has passed, we should consider our own need for rest, a period of time when we are not available, time for personal renewal and nurture.

28. *Ta Kuo* / *Preponderance of the Great*

Primary Trigrams

above *Tui* / The Joyous, Lake
below *Sun* / The Gentle, Wood, Wind

Nuclear Trigrams

above *Ch'ien* / The Creative, Heaven
below *Ch'ien* / The Creative, Heaven

The hexagram represents a great ridgepole or beam (four central yang lines) that is resting on slight and inadequate supports (two yin lines, bottom and top). This is a precarious, even dangerous, situation that must be remedied at once if collapse is to be avoided. While change must be initiated promptly, it should be with appropriate and careful attention; it is not a time to over-react or become agitated. The act of addressing the situation is what is important now, not what will follow.

The hexagram's structure emphasizes the theme of pushing resources as far as they can go, in that it resembles a candle being burned at both ends. No matter how worthwhile, creative, or exciting our lives or projects might be, they rely for their realization on our continuing well-being. The individual or situation represented by this hexagram is over-loaded and something needs to be reduced or released.

Letting go of something or somebody we have cherished is never easy, particularly if we remain identified with them in some way. This hexagram is associated with the theme of caring for the dead and the changing customs in China relating to above- or below-ground burial. For the individual who is facing this exceptional time and its tasks, part of the remedy may lie in looking at what needs to be 'buried', allowed to die. It may be that too much is wanting to be 'kept alive' in our lives and that something needs to be let go of, mourned, and allowed to pass on.

Balancing urgency with thoughtfulness and care presents a considerable challenge. We must hold our focus quietly and see the situation through to its resolution.

The Changing Lines

6/1st   If we are determined not to recognize a dangerous situation, we will always find ways to justify carrying on. The most difficult part of releasing an excessive burden is often simply acknowledging that it exists. Taking that step shows that we are prepared to address the situation. To ignore this counsel would be foolish, not courageous.

9/2nd The excessive burden referred to in this hexagram may be being carried not by us but by another. If we see this situation and do nothing, we fail ourselves as well as the other person. There is always something we can do. Of course, we may be so cut off from our own 'Other' that this failure of support is entirely self-contained. There is often an element of shame attached to not being able to carry a heavy load, and reaching out to others is the best way to counteract this possibility.

9/3rd   At times we are so far into a situation such as pictured here that we decide the only way out is through, that we must just lower our heads and soldier on. In a sense we are passing on the responsibility for balance to 'the Gods', and an exhausted collapse may be the outcome. Curiously, we may feel better about ourselves for handling it in this way rather than taking the responsibility ourselves. The heroic attitude does not loosen its grip easily.

9/4th   There may be another way of dealing with the exceptional circumstances that form the image of the times, and that could be to distribute the burden more widely so that it becomes the responsibility of all and possibly even of benefit to all. This possibility requires us to look afresh at the situation, to seek what may be its hidden potential.

9/5th   Discerning whether we are part of the problem or part of the solution is not always easy; we may think we are being helpful when we are just perpetuating the situation. If we find any rigidity inside ourselves, we should try to release it. Any situation can become an opportunity for learning and transformation, but we must first let go of the idea that we know what outcome is the most desirable.

6/top   The conditions that have shaped this period are drawing to a close. If we find that no sooner have we managed to survive one challenge than we find ourselves facing the next, we might need to consider why we continually attract apparently exceptional circumstances. In this case, the 'problem' has arisen because the two yin or yielding lines were having to bear four yang or firm lines. If yin energies are repeatedly asked to perform in the same way as yang energies, then the outcome will be the same – the danger of collapse. We should reflect on whether we are respecting and valuing the different qualities that yin and yang represent and, further, what our concept of wholeness is.

29. K'an / The Abysmal (Water) (The Deep, The Depths)

Primary Trigrams

above K'an / The Abysmal, Water
below K'an / The Abysmal, Water

Nuclear Trigrams

above Kên / Keeping Still, Mountain
below Chên / The Arousing, Thunder

K'an is associated with danger because it represents moving water, deep water, and ground water, which is water so deep that it has passed out of sight. The danger is not so much something to be overcome as it is a condition or circumstance to be recognized. The hexagram itself pictures an abyss or ravine, with a strong middle line lying between two yielding, or 'dark', lines representing the high banks or cliffs of a river or gorge. This is not a situation from which we can easily remove ourselves: we are in the water and we must get on with it, not fight it or deny it. That would only create danger of a different order.

The way to behave in these circumstances is to become at one with the element in which we find ourselves. Water moves; it flows and plunges and tumbles, never being held back for long. Responding to the pull of the moon, drawn to the sea, not resisting but flowing as its nature dictates that it must, the motion of water represents that which in the human sphere might be identified as a sort of fundamental trust, a willingness to lose oneself in the current of life, not to hold back or keep anything in reserve, 'just in case'. This is not a counsel for mindlessly abandoning ourselves to whatever current has the strongest pull; on the contrary, with wholehearted commitment to see the situation through, however hard it might be on us emotionally, we are committing ourselves to the work of the Creative in this moment. As the high cliffs confine the waters of

K'an in the imagery of this hexagram, forcing them to work through that channel and no other, so these times demand that we work with where we are, using the capacity we all possess to comprehend a situation on more than an intellectual level, to 'feel' our way into the very heart of it – as an explorer and as a lover.

The repetition of the trigram *K'an* indicates that the danger we are facing is not one that will pass in the ordinary way, but one that is inseparable from life itself, if we intend to live courageously. Our 'depths' are what make us human and interesting, the place where we are vulnerable and real. It is not surprising that the entire life cycle lies at the heart of this hexagram, between the nuclear trigrams *Chên*, the Arousing, and *Kên*, the Mountain, symbolizing all the beginnings and endings of life as well as the mystery that lies at its core.

A final note: in English usage the word 'abysmal' has lost its connection with its root, abyss, and is applied instead to describe, for instance, bad behaviour or an extremely poor performance. 'Dreadful' and 'awful' are two other words that have become detached from their roots and lost their original meaning. All these words point to the same type of overwhelming experience, numinous, frightening, charged with a sense of mystery and danger. *K'an* has been seen as the light of reason within the darkness of the material body, but this duality does not serve the breadth of the image well. Perhaps imagining it as representing the light of consciousness embedded in the limitless reaches of the collective unconscious conveys better the totality of the imagery.

The Changing Lines

6/1st   Danger exercises a fascination for many of us. Indeed, probably most of us would not want to live a life of constant, guaranteed safety. But between these two extremes lies a vast area of possible attitudes to danger – reckless, blind, fearful, exhilarated, challenged, courageous, naïve. The *I Ching* generally takes a moderate stance, and counsels a cautious and alert attitude, neither courting danger nor avoiding it. Perhaps there is no 'right' attitude, only the right awareness of what our particular attitude is so that we do not fool ourselves into situations in which we are 'out of

our depth' and must look to others for rescue and the impo-
sition of limits.

9/2nd This line represents the first expression of the powerful
movement addressed in the hexagram. It is reflected by the
strong line in the fifth position, and these two lines suggest
the deep flow of life and passion through time. This is not a
transient condition, nor is it limited to us alone. Rather than
contracting against the danger symbolized here by deep,
rapidly-flowing water, we need to learn how to step into it
and see where it takes us. This requires a gathered act of
calm commitment that neither over- nor under-exaggerates
the importance of this choice.

6/3rd There is always a risk, midway through an undertaking or
an adventure, that the momentum created by our forward
movement will push us on ill-advisedly. If it is time to stop,
if we are tired or impatient or in a dangerously heroic
mode, then we must stop and rest and perhaps review our
inner state of being. A more thoughtful approach may help
us to place ourselves and our contribution in a wider
context from which others will also benefit.

6/4th It is not always possible to act in anything like a measured
way in the face of danger, and we may find ourselves overwhelmed and exhausted by events before we have had time
to think or make a different choice. As in flood conditions,
we need to get out of the water and back on to dry land.
Failing that, we need to find something or somebody to
hang on to while we catch our breath. There may be nothing we can do until the waters themselves subside, in
which case we can, at least, stop struggling.

9/5th The action of water is immensely powerful over time, yet it
is utterly yielding from moment to moment; having no
movement of its own, it is drawn by the invisible force of
gravity both within the earth's field and from the more
distant pull of the moon. Our planet, and we ourselves, are
seventy per cent water, and yet we resist and fear our
'watery' nature, striving to stop the unceasing flow of life
and make things more solid and hard; similarly, we resist
or mistrust the pull of invisible – irrational – forces. Our
greatest resources lie in our depths.

6/top   The conditions and energies addressed by this hexagram are coming to a close. Now is the time to step away from the depths and move freely into a new balance. If this seems difficult, we may still be identified with or entangled by recent events. The lesson of water is relevant here: we need to simply move on, let go of where we have been and keep flowing.

30. Li / The Clinging, Fire

Primary Trigrams

above *Li* / The Clinging, Fire
below *Li* / The Clinging, Fire

Nuclear Trigrams

above *Tui* / The Joyous, Lake
below *Sun* / The Gentle, Wind, Wood

Of all the hexagrams representing the elements, *Li* is the most diffi-cult to comprehend, to articulate. In a sense, as with a flame, the best we can do is simply contemplate it and allow our minds to wander and then to return again and again to the focal image itself, its central emptiness, its almost non-existence. Fire is a process, not a thing; it moves; it consumes; it grows; it dies; it is rekindled again and again, always different, always the same. Beautiful, destructive, creative, brilliant, terrifying: it is, perhaps, the most evocative and powerful symbol for life that we have.

Many of these associations have to do with transience, and the hexagram contains within it further suggestions that *Li* refers to states of mind and being that are, by their very nature, ephemeral and contingent. Joy – *Tui* – arises and passes as do the reflections and disturbances on the surface of a lake. Wind – *Sun* – is here and gone, never lingering. Brevity often increases rather than decreases the potency of moments of intense experience, and their passing may be felt as a bereavement, or with profound relief.

Li represents clarity and radiance, in nature and in the human mind and spirit. It also signifies the eye and vision. If we wish to be 'enlightened', we must empty ourselves of preconceptions. The yielding line in the central position of both primary trigrams repre-sents this emptiness as well as the open and sincere attitude that accompanies the desire for enlightenment. The individual who has struggled for understanding and gained wisdom may become a light for others.

Without fuel, fire is just an idea; it has no existence separate from that to which it clings, that which nourishes it. The same is true of life, human, animal, and vegetable: all matter requires fuel for survival, and the quality and nature of the fuel that is chosen – or is available – will affect the quality and nature of the life sustained.

The Changing Lines

9/1st   As the first position in this hexagram of light or fire, we might consider this strong initial line to be representing sunrise. We should not allow ourselves to be swept up too quickly in the pressures and demands of the day, but to take something of the stillness of the night with us into the day, a 'gathered' spirit. If this is not possible and we do find ourselves moving quickly from one activity to another, we can at least try to safeguard our clarity of mind and not allow it to become dispersed or scattered.

6/2nd   This open line characterizes the energy of the hexagram of fire within a human being; it represents clarity, sincerity, lack of prejudice, brilliance. Whoever possesses these qualities has learned early on that cultivating an attitude of trust and curiosity towards life yields greater dividends than approaching each moment already 'full-up' with expectations, anxieties, or predetermined goals.

9/3rd   A great deal of the emphasis in this hexagram is on the quality of dynamic emptiness, how we nourish it, what we allow into it, how it affects others. On account of its use at the forge to strengthen and test metal, fire has come to represent truth, and truth, in human terms, must be 'fired' by honesty. We cannot force others to be honest, but we must strive for honesty with ourselves. We cannot hope to make enlightened choices if our decisions are clouded by half-truths and wishful thinking.

9/4th   'Make of yourself a light.' This is one interpretation of what were reputedly the Buddha's last words. As with the flame, so human radiance is paradoxical in that the relationship of form to content is irresolvable. Those who are truly radiant seem to be almost transparent and lack the edge of conceit that others who are striving to appear brilliant so often demonstrate. Seeking clarity and emptiness is a life-long path that may in time translate into radiance as perceived by others. It cannot be a goal in itself.

6/5th In the position of the ruler of the hexagram, this empty line represents all that we might associate with an enlightened individual, the ideal leader. Interestingly, such individuals rarely stand on ceremony or insist on deference or recognition. On the contrary, they seem to place particular value on the opportunities they have to live and enjoy the very ordinary pleasures of friends and family, of meeting new people, sharing, and laughing. Their priorities are for quiet time to reflect and enjoy the natural world and time to warm themselves at the 'fire' of human relationships.

9/top The nature of fire is both creative and destructive; some seeds lie dormant until a fierce enough fire frees them to germinate. The lesson for us is that we should not try to restrict or hang on to the movements of life that bring us good times. What we cannot see, we find hard to imagine; it is only by loosening our grip on our limited goals that we will free ourselves to experience greater possibilities.

31. Hsien / Influence (Wooing)

Primary Trigrams

above *Tui* / The Joyous, Lake
below *Kên* / Keeping Still, Mountain

Nuclear Trigrams

above *Ch'ien* / The Creative, Heaven
below *Sun* / The Gentle, Wind, Wood

As soon as we are born our ability to influence others will determine how and if we survive. If our signals of need are responded
to with recognition and care, then we are likely to experience both
a sense of relief and perhaps even a primitive form of gratitude. If,
on the other hand, our early attempts to recruit necessary attention
are continually met with impatience, harshness, or indifference, the
experience of relationship may be shaped by fear and suspicious-
ness and enacted through power struggles rather than mutuality.
The development of self-esteem and the capacity to represent
ourselves effectively in the 'outside' world have their roots in these
earliest experiences.

The dynamic represented by this hexagram is, in effect, driven
by desire, but mutuality – the benefit gained from give-and-take –
is also suggested. The youngest daughter, *Tui*, is being courted by
the youngest son, *Kên*. The image suggests a relatively uncomplicated and happy romantic and erotic engagement. Although it is
not necessarily an enduring union, this is what is said to 'make the
world go round'. The theme of benevolent influence arises from the
images associated with the primary trigrams, that is, the Mountain
with a lake at its summit. The Lake is seen to benefit or stimulate
the mountain because it provides moisture for all creatures who live
there, and the Mountain is seen to benefit the lake because it attracts
clouds that fill the lake with rain. In addition, the gentle 'willing-

ness' of the mountain to sacrifice its peak so that the lake can form and reflect Heaven gives another focus for reflecting on how, at its best, influence works to the benefit of all.

We need to think carefully about what sort of influence, what sort of recognition or effect, we wish to have and why. Relationships, whether with others or with ourselves, that are based on trust will not necessarily be repaid with trust, but those based on mistrust, fear, or manipulation will surely turn sour. We should be prepared to approach others (or to approach our projects) free of prejudice or the intention to exploit. This is about openness and sincerity, not naïveté. It is only through emptying oneself that others, perceiving our receptivity, will feel free to approach.

In brief, this hexagram is about getting on in the world, growing up, making a relationship with 'reality', with work, ambition, and human interactions of all sorts.

The Changing Lines

6/1st The nature of relationships is such that we may, at times, provoke a 'show-down' in order to get a hidden conflict or difference of opinion out into the open where it can be addressed. In general, a gentler approach is probably better, as provocation is a form of manipulation and can be both hurtful and disrespectful. A related situation may present itself where inherent differences do not resolve themselves over time and lead, instead, to a parting of the ways. The degree of change that any particular relationship can tolerate in one 'partner' or another varies. As the first position in the hexagram, whatever actions or attitudes are present, the situation is still in its early stages.

6/2nd If we conducted all our relationships with the same degree of careful attention and thoughtfulness as we apply to the early stages of a hoped-for romantic liaison, our intuition and sensitivity would grow wonderfully and the relationships themselves would flourish. Instead, we are likely either to take them for granted or to over-burden them with hopes and fears that are often unrelated to the present. We are essentially fragile creatures, prone to worry, and lacking self-confidence, and we should recognize how precious and how delicate our capacity to make and sustain relationships is. If we valued them more we would take better care of them.

9/3rd   'Influence' implies an effort to get right inside another person, into their heart and thoughts, under their skin. The aim is to direct their choices towards a goal chosen by the person who is exerting the influence. This is not the ideal way for individuals to come together, as an element of force is involved, even if it is slight. None the less, we all seek to persuade or influence others at times. We would do well to reflect on the degree of resistance we are seeking to overcome and whether the course of action that we are encouraging is really congruent with the nature and goals of the other person.

9/4th   There is really no way to establish relationships of any depth without going into our own inner depths. Human beings are complex, and we delude ourselves if we believe we know or understand another person completely. If we draw back when things become complicated or unpredictable, our hearts learn to close rather than to open.

9/5th   Sometimes we find ourselves needing to engage with individuals with whom it is difficult to establish a connection that works. We seem not to be 'on the same wave-length' or able to pull together in order to achieve an objective. This can also be true at times of our self-relating, when we seem to be at odds with ourselves. While confusion persists we do well to not force the issue, but rather to modify our expectations and stay as centred as possible.

6/top   Relationships based on mutual attraction are at their most dynamic when the flow of energies is reciprocal and there is a true affinity that underlies what may be considered more circumstantial reasons for attraction. None the less, even such a powerful connection will inevitably reach its peak and then begin to change, making space for complementary but possibly very different ways of being. While this may present a challenge, it is a perfectly natural movement.

32. Hêng / Duration

Primary Trigrams

above *Chên* / The Arousing, Thunder
below *Sun* / The Gentle, Wind

Nuclear Trigrams

above *Tui* / The Joyous, Lake
below *Ch'ien* / The Creative, Heaven

There are two aspects to Duration as reflected in this hexagram. On the one hand, there are the 'givens' of nature, our own and that of the universe within which we live. The Tao has its own laws of increase and decrease, growth and decay, and these endure, as do the laws governing human life and human activity. On the other hand, as human beings we need to learn how to endure the challenges and vicissitudes of life without being crushed by them or becoming so passive in the face of them that we simply allow ourselves to be blown about as a bit of grass is in the wind, or become brutalized so that we elect just to lower our heads and plough on blindly. To endure requires a capacity not only to stay in place but also to provide a resource for oneself, a means of nurturing oneself; it involves working with and limiting one's despair or bitterness, waiting for the next breath, keeping some seed fresh and ready for the moment when conditions alter.

The breath is often the focus for meditation practice because the simple alternation of inhalation and exhalation is calming both physically and mentally. Rumi writes movingly of this alternation in the poem 'Birdwings' (Barks & Moyne, 1995):

'Your deepest presence is in every small contracting and expanding,
the two as beautifully balanced and coordinated as birdwings'

Throughout life we 'inhale', taking the world in, and then we 'exhale', releasing it, surrendering ourselves. At times when we feel we are being asked to endure more than is bearable, we need to remember that to live we must breathe – in and out – and to endure we must learn likewise that there is a time for holding on and a time for letting go.

There is a reflection of this principle in the lines: all the lines in the two primary trigrams correspond; that is, for every yielding line in the lower trigram, there is a corresponding firm line in the upper, and for every firm line in the lower, there is a corresponding yielding line in the upper. Breathing out and breathing in. And for this reason the condition of marriage is also associated with this hexagram, being the union of complementarities. *Chên* is the oldest son and *Sun* the oldest daughter, and this leads to marriage as a central theme in this hexagram. (This is an important distinction between this hexagram and the previous one.) By its very nature the marriage relationship (or long-term relationships, in general) involve the shared experience of births and deaths, gains and losses, the journey through life towards old age and death. Love must grow and change, or it will die and become indifference. Anger, misunderstanding, conflict, joy, friendship, intimacy, forgiveness, sorrow, gratitude, and, one hopes, acceptance are all waves that will move through and, occasionally perhaps, threaten to drown the marriage partners.

The Changing Lines

6/1st If, as suggested by this hexagram, the balance of energies is particularly important at this time in order to sustain ourselves or our relationships through time, then impulsive or hasty initiatives are both unnecessary and also unhelpful, in that they create an imbalance from the outset. Such actions probably reflect a lack of trust in the slower pace of natural processes, but, by forcing the pace, they set in motion a dynamic that may need to be corrected sooner rather than later.

9/2nd Difficult times test and shape us, and we may need to draw on reserves of courage and patience that we did not know existed. Living one day at a time, even one hour at a time, is the way to endure; if we multiply the demands of the present by all the days and weeks that lie ahead we will quickly feel overwhelmed.

9/3rd Relationships that endure and deepen over time develop a capacity for subtle shifts and adaptations in their dynamic. Confrontation can be creative and is necessary at times, but it is exhausting if every difference of opinion leads to a struggle and creates a competition in which only one person can 'win'. Somehow, difference must be accepted and enjoyed rather than becoming an excuse for the explosive discharge of feelings. Working with conflict and learning to trust that difference need not be dangerous is a life-long education.

9/4th Duration, the name of this hexagram, implies the passage of time. Some efforts bear fruit early and encourage us to continue; others do not 'ripen' for a long time and can lead to frustration and doubt, even to our losing faith in our original vision. If we are assailed by such feelings, simply breathing in and out while letting go of inner critical or frightened thoughts can reconnect us to the basic rhythm of life and reaffirm our willingness to persevere without knowing where the process will take us or what it will require of us.

6/5th In the strong fifth position we would ordinarily expect to find a firm, yang line; instead, we find a yielding one. It is interesting to consider the relationship and interplay between the two qualities of, first, endurance, a capacity associated with the feminine throughout the ages, and, second, strength or power, an attribute associated with the masculine. Confusing these two qualities may lead us to undertake more than we can manage or to attempt to sustain an effort that was only appropriate in the short-term. If we find ourselves in this position, we should be wise rather than heroic and take time to rest and reflect on our priorities.

6/top Those who take on responsibility – great or small – with a quiet determination to see things through to their conclusion contribute a great deal to the common good. In the end we are all responsible for the culture that we create around us, and whether or not we contribute something of lasting value is up to us.

33. Tun / Retreat

Primary Trigrams

above *Ch'ien* / The Creative, Heaven
below *Kên* / Keeping Still, Mountain

Nuclear Trigrams

above *Ch'ien* / The Creative, Heaven
below *Sun* / The Gentle, Wind, Wood

This is a calendar hexagram representing the sixth month of the Chinese calendar, July–August, when the summer solstice is past and the days are beginning to shorten towards the autumn and winter. The lines reflect this change in energy, in that the yin lines, the lines of darkness, are beginning to rise up into the hexagram, displacing the yang or light lines. We may not notice it at this point – often the warmth of the summer lingers in the air or water for months – but a shift has occurred and we probably sense it on some level, even if we are not consciously aware of it.

The theme of the hexagram is suggested by the image of the mountain below and the heavens above: we may climb a mountain because we find the challenge and achievement exciting and life-affirming, or simply because we enjoy the experience and appreciate the view at the end of it. Whatever our motivation, the time comes when we find ourselves at the top and can go no further. Still the heavens extend (or retreat) infinitely beyond our sight and beyond our reach. The only way forward is down. It might even become dangerous to remain stubbornly on the top of the mountain, frustrated or angry that we had no further to go. Under these circumstances recognition of the requirements of the time involves a shift of energy and attention. We need to become still like the mountain and think creatively and penetratingly about the timing and manner of the descent. Then the retreat down the mountain is simply part of the wholeness of the experience, coming back to earth, becoming grounded again. This is not a defeat, it is the appropriate response to the particular situation and time.

In the west we seldom recognize the wisdom of an appropriate and timely retreat. Retreat is seen as cowardly or lazy; periods of retreat are permissible only in a religious context. We tire ourselves out with continual advancement and seem to fear a loss of momentum or cessation of motion as if it were death itself. Perhaps we equate our continuing well-being, almost our identity, with being able to give a 'progress report' that shows we are always on the move, never looking back, never retracing our footsteps. This hexagram reminds us of the importance of recognizing when the time has come to retreat, when the times themselves are not congruent with persistent movement in one direction (or medium: the earth of the mountain becomes the air of the heavens). This may be a time to accept more depressive energies, to come down from a high point of achievement or enjoyment, perhaps even to face something that we climbed the mountain to avoid. More broadly, the hexagram points to the wisdom of recognizing limits and limitations, learning from the natural imagery of mountain and sky and from the cycles of the seasons that all things change and are diminished or increased in turn. If we struggle against or fear these natural laws, we will only cause ourselves to suffer. If we accept them and yield to their effects, we will find a deeper certainty.

The Changing Lines

6/1st The times represented by this hexagram are characterized by the need to recognize when we have gone as far as we can go in a particular direction. The sooner we recognize this, the better; we can stop and consider the circumstances with an open mind and perhaps consult with others whom we trust and who share something of our vision or goals. We should be prepared to completely abandon our current course, if necessary. Only by being willing to release everything will we be able to see other, new possibilities.

6/2nd Nostalgia can paralyse us and create a painful sense of regret and loss that erases the present and its goodness and aliveness. Such feelings often coincide with the onset of autumn and the decreasing light. This retreat from the present and what 'is' can be remarkably hard to shift and constitutes a real obstacle to the flow of energy necessary for facing the advance of a different 'season' with different demands.

9/3rd We are never invulnerable to all the drives and feelings that shape human life. We learn through mistakes and we learn by watching others. At times we feel we have learnt nothing and have it all to do again. The Chinese saying, 'You never step in the same stream twice', can be helpful at these times; life flows on and the more we can let go of yesterday's flow and step into today's, the more free will we be to experiment and live creatively.

9/4th Preconceived ideas about ourselves and what success or achievement looks like can hinder our natural growth and make it more difficult for us to find our own, unique form and path. If we find we are experiencing life as empty or life-denying, we should look carefully at how we might be limiting our vision ourselves and try to gently open up again to the flow of life.

9/5th There is a sense in which we must continually relinquish our search for security and certainty and seek, instead, clarity and a quiet heart. Imagining that the answer lies someplace else, or that we will find ourselves when we achieve one more goal, places the emphasis on There and Then, rather than Here and Now. This is retreat as release from the fruitless search for a better Me or a better time.

9/top The seamlessness of change from season to season can teach us a lot about life. The new buds of spring are already present on winter branches; no sooner does the summer growth reach its peak than it begins its decline. The names we give things create an impression of the separateness of creatures and processes when, in fact, we are all interconnected and interdependent. Wisdom requires us to continually release our ideas of the solidity of things and to trust, instead, in the sheer creativity and aliveness of life.

34. Ta Chuang / The Power of the Great

Primary Trigrams

above *Chên* / The Arousing, Thunder
below *Ch'ien* / The Creative, Heaven

Nuclear Trigrams

above *Tui* / The Joyous, Lake
below *Ch'ien* / The Creative, Heaven

The season represented by this hexagram is spring. The hours of light are longer than those of dark and the warmth of the sun causes everything to break into blossom. At this season our senses are filled with the sights and sounds and scents of newness, of promise. The sap rises. It is not a time for caution or doubt; the season is brief and we would be foolish to resist it.[1] The dangers at such a time are those of a sort of intoxication, an identification with the powerful flow of seasonal energy that may result in the individual feeling that it is personal strength that has brought about the good times, rather than that it is in the nature of the cycles of being – human and cosmic – that such a time arises. Under these circumstances it is possible that we may become inflated with a sense of our own power or 'rightness' (or, worse still, righteousness), losing touch with the deeper levels of the Self and the Way, even wilfully ignoring reminders of our dependence on energies and forces greater than ourselves. The hexagram 'The Taming Power of the Great' (see Hexagram 26, *Ta Chu*) is similar to this one in that light lines are rising strongly, but there the lines are restrained by the upper trigram *Kên*, Mountain. The goal there is wisdom, and the point is that power restrained becomes truly formidable. Here, there is no goal apart from reaching the top, and no mention of the transformative effect of keeping still.

An alternative approach to the imagery of this hexagram suggests that the top two yin lines represent rain and the four yang lines represent the ridgepole of a roof. While the earliest human beings would have welcomed the shelter provided by caves and guarded it jealously, later humans were able to construct their own shelters, thus gaining much greater independence from the natural world and protection against its vagaries. A sense of power accompanies any advance that raises us above the level of basic existence, and this can lead to viewing ourselves as somehow separate from the rest of the natural world, less affected by it, less responsible for it. This is a lonely and possibly dangerous position.

The hexagram 'The Power of the Great' illustrates the complexity of times when personal strength and creativity – acting in harmony with nature – flourish. Both approaches to the imagery and associations of the hexagram recognize the importance of human effort and achievement. The emphasis here is on a lack of balance that may begin to harden the energy flow, making it into something more driven. We are wise to pause at such a time, reflecting deeply on how these considerations might apply to the questions or area of concern that we brought to the *I Ching*.

The Changing Lines

9/1st All power must be grounded if it is to last and to be of enduring value. Many statues of the Buddha show him touching the earth with the fingers of one hand, reflecting the importance of this truth. Given the energies that inform this time, we do well to adopt an open and receptive attitude towards events and possibilities, not doubting our strength and the promise of the times but being prepared to move slowly and steadily, without haste and keeping our feet on the ground.

9/2nd Power without vision can be dangerous. In order to create space for envisioning where we are going and why, we must find or make time to approach these questions honestly. If we simply allow ourselves to be carried on the wave of energy as it builds, without any sense of direction or limitation, we might find ourselves tossed aside or 'high and dry' when it finally breaks. Now may be the best time to pause, not only to consider these questions, but also to appreciate the goodness of that which already exists.

9/3rd Being near the growing edge of change and growth can be very exciting, feeling part of something bigger than oneself, particularly if this movement is fuelled by idealism and hopes for profound change. We must bear in mind, however, that we may easily become unbalanced by this dynamic and lose sight of our own needs and goals. A naïve or irresponsible attitude will not serve us well.

9/4th The sense of having reached a 'point of no return' can act as a bell rung to wake us up, and we may suddenly find ourselves becoming anxious about where a particular movement or energy is taking us, whereas before we were relatively complacent. We have a choice: we can pull out altogether, we can step back from the situation and find our footing again before moving forward, or we can move into the unknown with a balance of curiosity and caution. There is not one 'right' way; each situation must be approached afresh.

6/5th A time may come when we recognize the fragility of both life and power, when we view our accumulated 'wealth' or influence or experience from a different perspective and have the opportunity to re-evaluate it. There may still be the temptation to identify with the greatness (or 'littleness') of it, to fear the changes that would accompany the loss or release of it, the opening of a new chapter of our lives. 'Greatness' will be redefined many times during the course of a lifetime.

6/top It can be difficult to bear feelings of envy or exclusion if we feel good fortune is coming to others but not to us. A sense of isolation may creep in, further intensifying such feelings. We must consciously move away from this experience and, instead, cultivate a different sort of awareness, one that centres us quietly in our own strength. This may require a determined effort but it is essential to persevere.

Note

1. The circumstances of spring in the northern hemisphere obviously do not apply in the southern. Nor, in fact, do the comments regarding the

speed or character of seasonal change apply at all latitudes and longitudes. The *I Ching* takes the imagery of seasons as a starting point for reflections that apply to the movements of nature and the human heart. For example, 'spring' is not confined to any particular month; it is a designation that can be applied to any 'spring-like' movement of energy. While this hexagram is associated with the second month of the Chinese calendar, March–April, this is only an incidental 'fact' and should not limit the hexagram's interpretation in any way.

35. Chin / Progress

Primary Trigrams

above *Li* / The Clinging, Fire
below *K'un* / The Receptive, Earth

Nuclear Trigrams

above *K'an* / The Abysmal, Water
below *Kên* / Keeping Still, Mountain

The sun rises over the earth without hindrance. If we cannot see it, it may be because we are indoors or it may be because there are clouds lying between us and the sun. The appearance of the sun moving through the sky is, of course, an illusion created by our own movement as the earth rotates around that body. Progress through life is similarly open to misinterpretation, frequently harmless, occasionally dangerous. We can only measure our progress against something or somebody else. Comparison is inherent in the concept and comparisons are always to the advantage or disadvantage of one or the other party. Perhaps we need reminding from time to time that we should make the most of the time we have now, this day, this moment and not waste time in imagining a better day to come. The Latin phrase, *Carpe diem* translates as 'Seize the day' (more colloquially, 'Go for it!').

Naturally, we would like to know how to create the conditions that make progress possible. As always, the answer lies in recognizing and understanding the energies inherent in the present moment and aligning oneself with them. Here we have the brilliant energy of fire, *Li*, which represents the eye, clarity of vision and judgement, as well as sincerity and truth. *Li* is 'empty' or yielding in the middle, indicating a temperament that is not self-seeking or egotistical but is, rather, willing to listen and receive the views of others, a lack of rigidity. Below *Li*, in the hexagram, lies the trigram of *K'un*, representing the earth, the people, receptivity, and devotion. There are no obstacles here that might prevent or obstruct the energy of *Li*; on the contrary, there is a resource – the respect and support of others. These two energies are informed (literally, formed from within) by the attributes of courage in the face of danger (*K'an* representing the depths, the heart, sorrow, as well as the willingness to 'plunge in', even if doing so may take one into unknown areas) and a capacity for stillness and reflection (*Kên*, the Mountain). From this it is clear that the apparently effortless progress represented by the sun rising over the earth in this hexagram has been achieved through a combination of vision, courage, reflection, and, importantly, the support and respect of one's fellow human beings.

Another consideration raised by this hexagram is that of work. We must all 'earn' our living, even if we are not in paid employment. We earn it by living with as much awareness of the interconnectedness of life as we are able, reflecting on whether we are part of the solution to the sufferings and needs of the world or part of the problem. We are shaped by our work, and while many (perhaps most) people on the planet have no choice about the work they must do to live, those of us who are more able to choose probably also have a greater influence on the overall distribution of wealth and resources. The choices we make around work will contribute fundamentally to the point of balance we seek to maintain in life.

The Changing Lines

6/1st   Whatever path we are pursuing, if we wish to make headway we must commit ourselves to the process on a daily basis. There is a discipline inherent in progress that must be embraced and observed or we risk derailment by the first challenge.

6/2nd Living and breathing in the present moment is the precondition for all effective action. We are, then, firmly grounded in our bodies and in our actual circumstances. While we must be able to think clearly, this is not a separate activity from being aware of our deepest feelings. Good judgement proceeds from this combined awareness.

6/3rd   By definition there is nothing more transitory than progress. We cannot stop it or control it, but we can learn to live with it, not taking it for granted but enjoying its fruits when they are offered. We are wise to share those fruits with others and to exercise restraint in speaking of good fortune or hard times. Everything passes and we may well find ourselves looking to others for support or respect under different circumstances.

9/4th   The indivisible yang and yin of progress are clarity and awareness, on the one hand, and a willingness to let go of knowing and understanding on the other. It is in the nature of all processes that they lead us into shadowy and even dark places where the concept of progress is no longer applicable. The practice then is one of patience and receptivity. There is no reason to feel isolated or victimized, however, as 'waiting and seeing' is what most of us are doing most of the time.

6/5th   Sometimes it is not easy to identify why things are going well; we may look to our obvious strengths to explain it, but in doing so we could miss the power of the 'earth' elements. In this hexagram, the yielding energies outnumber the firm ones; this could point to the importance of those who support us, or to a generous capacity for patience and openness, or to a willingness to limit growth in the interest of balance. If the balance shifts to a more rigid or driven mode, we might find that we gradually lose momentum, lose our way. Once recognized, this can be addressed.

9/top   When we are attempting to hold many threads together without neglecting our work or our responsibilities to others, we may find it increasingly difficult to have any sense of positive development. Life is reduced to hanging on, and we may well lose our enthusiasm for almost everything. If we can accept this as simply part of the continuing 'tidal' movement of life and not make things harder for ourselves by self-criticism, we may find that others will come forward to generate movement or take on responsibility. The hexagram pictures the sun moving over the earth during the course of the day. By the time we reach this, the last line, we are moving towards dusk. 'Sufficient unto the day is the evil thereof.'

36. Ming I / Darkening of the Light ('Wounding of the Bright')

Primary Trigrams

above *K'un* / The Receptive, Earth
below *Li* / The Clinging, Fire

Nuclear Trigrams

above *Chên* / The Arousing, Thunder
below *K'an* / The Abysmal, Water

The hexagram pictures light or fire beneath and within the earth, and this image is powerfully reflected in the title. The entire hexagram refers to the historical period in which King Wên (who wrote the judgements on the hexagrams) was imprisoned and his life in danger. Under these circumstances it was imperative that he should behave inconspicuously while doing all he could to endure and keep his spirit from failing. There is no harm in comparing our own struggles with those of King Wên; we can learn much about surviving adversity from his story.

Throughout life there may be times and circumstances in which it is advisable to hide our light, times in which we have not actively sought to be involved but have, none the less, been caught up. These events may be the result of greed, malice, or envy on the part of others. There are times when, no matter how well-behaved we are, there are still those who wish us harm or who just do not like us. However, we need to be aware that, without intending to do so, it is possible to contribute to the setting up of situations in which we shine too brightly and thus attract to ourselves these dangerous responses. This is, perhaps, why the Chinese always reserve their highest praise for the person who behaves modestly. Our behaviour at such times requires patience, forbearance, and trust in the ever-changing patterns of life and its energies. It is wise not to make our perseverance or endurance too obvious, however, or this, too, may attract anger and act as a provocation to further injury. This is not a counsel for masochistic submission to the situation, but rather for acceptance of it as it is, and for a quiet determination that we will outlast the period of adversity while safeguarding our sense of self.

The image of 'darkened' light or of 'injured' brightness is a powerful one, resonant with echoes of the eternal struggle between good and evil. We need to remember that this struggle is enacted through human lives and choices. For this reason we must always address the dark and the light within before we assign these qualities to external events and individuals. None the less, there are times when this struggle seems to be working itself out on a larger canvas. As individuals we have a responsibility as witnesses (perhaps as participants) not to turn away from injustice on account of our helplessness, protesting that there is nothing we can do.

Finally, there are times when we must dig deep inside ourselves and find a greatness equal to the challenge we face. It may be that we have not yet found our personal 'fire', not yet grasped our individuality or connected with our own vision. Perhaps this is the time to do so.

The Changing Lines

9/1st   The sooner we recognize and join the flow of the times the less we will need to struggle to find our way. When times are trying we do well to set aside our immediate plans and accept that forces much greater than our own will are at work. If we can simplify our requirements, reconnect with the ordinary rhythms of life and allow ourselves to be curious about what will happen next, this period will pass and we will have learnt something of value. If we waste our time in noisy frustration or grievance, we will attract the sort of attention that, at a later stage, we might very well not welcome.

6/2nd   This is the defining line of the hexagram and we are dealing with a paradox: how can we understand the energies of the time if openness and sincerity must be hidden? Ambiguity permeates the situation: how do we know what or whom to trust? Must we dissemble, pretend to be something we are not? Perhaps we need to use the perceptiveness associated with this line to gain insight into our own balance at such a time. There may be an element of naïveté in our attitude, and that is something we can identify and correct. We must be sure not to remain hidden beyond the period indicated by necessity.

9/3rd There is a time for contraction and concentration and careful behaviour and it will draw to a natural close and then begin to move into a more expansive time. This is the way the rhythms of life move. We must be attentive to these shifting energies, not rushing them and not obstructing them. If periods of difficulty have given us a sense of purpose or strength, we may find ourselves feeling a bit lost when the picture changes. It takes time to find a new balance.

6/4th This line represents the moment that the situation begins to move out of the sphere of danger and to enter a new period of movement. There is promise in the air. Hard times require us to focus and to simplify, and we may even prefer this to the complexity of choice and demand that accompanies a less obviously stressful life. None the less, we instinctively celebrate the moment when we can again breathe easily and deeply, experiencing the real pleasure of being alive.

6/5th Sometimes one small change effected with quiet commitment can alter a situation that had seemed irredeemable. The creation of a more balanced or integrated relationship between the 'light' and the 'dark' is neither achieved nor sustained effortlessly, however. Now the process of closure requires careful and thoughtful attention to detail. It is not a time to rush into the next challenge on a wave of triumph and adrenalin.

6/top By yielding to the demands of the times, rather than struggling against them, we may discover an inner stillness and strength that will enable us to survive. When those times have passed the challenge will be to allow ourselves to become more 'visible', to embody and integrate what we have learnt into a more balanced and ordinary way of life. As this line changes, the image becomes that of fire contained within the mountain rather than hidden beneath the earth. (See Hexagram 22, *Pi* / Grace).

37. Chia Jên / The Family (The Clan)

Primary Trigrams

above *Sun* / The Gentle, Wind, Wood
below *Li* / The Clinging, Fire

Nuclear Trigrams

above *Li* / The Clinging, Fire
below *K'an* / The Abysmal, Water

The family is the most powerful institution in society in terms of the formation of the individual. In this way we can say that the influence of the family is similar to that of a fire that burns brightly and can be seen from far away. Fire has the dual aspect of something warming and protective against the dangers of what lives or lurks beyond its circle and also something which is potentially destructive, which can get out of control, sucking air into itself with greater and greater energy, creating the phenomena of fire-storms, hugely powerful, hungry for fuel.

In the same way, the family may be a source of comfort, nurture, and culture (fire was the essential first step towards culture) or it may be consuming, destructive, a trap, a claustrum. Functional or dysfunctional, the family is our first experience and one that we will carry within ourselves and that will shape our own relationships throughout life.

The nature of relationships within the family was firmly prescribed in China, with an intensely masculine and hierarchical prejudice. The woman was the centre of the household and was not expected to have any role beyond it. Her duties were clear and her allegiance to the word and will of her husband was expected to be total and unquestioning. The duties of each son were equally clear, and seniority defined these roles without reference to individual endowment, choice, or personality. Daughters also were ranked according to age, and otherwise were not considered worthy of mention. They would become wives in time and that was that.

We now view these attitudes as not only outdated but also repressive, even cruel. None the less, the family remains as important as ever, and our experiences of the sort of mother or father or sister or brother or family 'system' in which we grew up will continue to affect us. If some sort of understandable authority is experienced, if the parents make an effort to understand and value each child and each other, if there is a sense of the family relating to the greater whole of society in a creative or 'real' way, if life appears to be meaningful and, on the whole, worth living, then the family will generate a 'fire' that is fairly constructive and those who go out into the world from such a family will, by and large, be equipped to contribute to, enjoy, and challenge that world and themselves. Clarity, rather than chaos, usually helps children, as long as it is not rigid or unfeeling or insensitive to the individual and her needs and gifts.

The roles of father and mother, sister and brother are archetypally determined; that is, the deep structures and patterns of millions of years of fathering and mothering have created a readiness within for parents and siblings to behave in a particular way. The word 'Father' creates an instant image and expectation as well as perhaps conjuring up the personal father. The same will be true for the word 'Mother', as well as for 'Family'. If, in a particular family, the father or mother is 'missing', or the child is an 'only child', then a range of experience will be absent and that individual may go out into the world with a sort of yearning to fill the space in which the archetypal expectation of a particular relationship was never satisfied. These deep in-built patterns will be altered and shaped by our personal experiences, but they are there before the personal experience; they are older than any of us. For this reason, too, the influence of the family is great: it is like an iceberg where the part above water is our personal family and reaching down below to a great depth is the archetypal form of 'Family'; it is much bigger than one might think, and much more dangerous.

The eight 'foundation' trigrams reflect the essential nature of the family and constitute a sort of family themselves. In all their permutations, the yin of the female element and the yang of the male create the three sons and three daughters, each a particular and specific mixture of 'mother' and 'father'. This full 'family' creates the conditions for all experiences of the elemental nature of the world and of humanity.

All in all, the family is the place we begin, the place that shapes us, the place we must leave, and the place that we must replicate within ourselves as well as within our own family 'of choice', in time.

The Changing Lines

9/1st   Whether our circumstances are supportive of, or obstructive to, growth will act as a major determinant of development, but equally – if not more – important is the unpredictable, inherent, and individual faculty or facility of each of us to benefit from, or adapt to, those circumstances. The 'fit', or lack of it, between the individual and the environment may be nurturing, challenging, or defeating. Where and how we get 'rooted' in life, whether it is in a sense that the world is basically a safe enough place to take risks or in the view that life is cruel and one should never risk exposure, will shape our capacity to trust and to dream.

6/2nd   Although yielding and moderate, this yin line – 'empty' as the flame is at its centre – represents the least visible but, perhaps, most essential person or aspect of the situation. Traditionally, the wife and mother was seen as this person within the family, almost without needs of her own, but responsible for the coherence of the whole. If unresolved resentment or grievance infects the role of nurturer, it can poison a situation. Conversely, when this role is embraced with joy and strength, it has the effect of re-establishing the feminine principle as the indivisible equal of the masculine.

9/3rd   In adolescence we are driven by passions that rise up and demand expression. Traditionally, this fierce but valuable energy was recognized through rites of passage that signalled the end of childhood and the beginning of adulthood, with all that that implied. We can be seized by this restless, hungry, impatient energy at any time in life, and whether we manage it wisely or harshly may reflect earlier experiences. At such times, access to a respected elder or teacher, either within or without, may enable us to open to the promise of the times while containing our impatience for change. Another approach might be to create a personal rite of passage to honour the potential of a new way of being in the world.

6/4th   Moving into the world from the base of the family may be a relief, an adventure, or an unwelcome challenge, and this can be true when we leave any situation, separating ourselves from something that has become too comfortable or too restrictive, when it no longer tests or nurtures us. Whether voluntary or involuntary, moving into the unknown and the strange requires gentleness, courage, and a willingness to create new and open relationships.

9/5th   Traditionally, this position is associated with the father, who was considered to be the 'head' of the family. It could also represent whatever principle or role we consider best reflects our image of ourselves. As a central authority figure – whether within a family, within the psyche, or within a more external situation – the responsibilities we bear and the repercussions of our choices are considerable. The balance we strike between decisiveness and openness or gentleness will shape the overall ethos of trust or mistrust. We must be particularly conscientious in not allowing authority to go to our heads, in not becoming identified with the role that has been assigned to us. We need to remain quietly in touch with our ordinariness.

9/top   Our definition of 'family' widens throughout life to include, finally, all those with whom we share this planet, even this universe. It stretches from before our time into the future. In order to grow into this realization we must learn to let go of all definitions over and over again, but we must also learn to recognize our own wholeness and the wholeness of every other individual being at every moment. Above all, we must learn to stop and pause and breathe and listen.

38. K'uei / Opposition

Primary Trigrams

above *Li* / The Clinging, Fire
below *Tui* / The Joyous, Lake

Nuclear Trigrams

above *K'an* / The Abysmal, Water
below *Li* / The Clinging, Fire

The elements that comprise the hexagram of Opposition are fire (*Li*) and contained water (*Tui*). By nature they are opposed, in that water can extinguish fire and fire can cause water to boil and evaporate. In order to safeguard the valuable qualities of each element they must be handled appropriately and with care. In the context of the present situation, fire and water represent apparent opposites that may have been, or are in danger of being, mishandled or misunderstood, resulting in confusion and conflict. If we fail to recognize the individual and particular nature of people or experiences, we can create misunderstanding and polarization that ends in estrangement and isolation. There are times, and they are not infrequent, when differences, while they cannot be resolved, must be acknowledged, respected, and taken into account. Even 'agreeing to differ' helps to bridge an inherent difference of opinion or approach.

This hexagram is relevant to times when there is not open conflict or a question of a lack of love, as in hexagram 6, *Sung* / Conflict. Neither is it similar to the hexagram representing *Revolution* (49, *Ko*), where the same two energies – *Li* and *Tui* – are reversed in the order in which they occur in the hexagram, creating the image of fire under water rather than above it. In that case there is much greater energy in the hexagram, leading to real change. None the less, the situation pictured in the present hexagram is one of painful alienation and disturbance in relationships, and under such circumstances major undertakings are to be avoided and smaller or closer goals should be contemplated instead.

This counsel guards against discharging the discomfort of the time by investing emotional, physical, or mental energy in extravagant schemes. The value of such a time lies in the work that is required to recognize and accommodate difference; it lies in the careful attention we must pay to the movements of our thoughts and feelings if we wish to gain a deeper understanding of ourselves and of the situation. While it is true that sometimes we can only discover what we are through recognizing what we are not, at this particular moment – when our ability to see clearly is most important – we may find ourselves in the grip of convictions that turn out to be distortions. If we can be slow to judge and compassionate towards ourselves and others, then understanding, when it does come, need not be accompanied by shame or regret.

Everything that has been said in terms of external confusion or misunderstanding applies equally to our inner conflicts: we ourselves are often pulled in different directions by the opposing tendencies of our nature and, at times, it may feel as if we will be torn apart by conflicting needs and desires. But if we can continue to name and bear these conflicts without trying to resolve, deny, or trivialize them, a third way may appear, and the confusion and disturbance that felt unbearable will seem to have disappeared almost miraculously.

Finally, human life is defined and conditioned by the opposites. Our earliest experiences are of yes and no, 'good' and 'bad', night and day, hot and cold, me and not-me. Through seeking to cultivate awareness, we can learn to expand our definitions to recognize conditioning for what it is: the shaping of an individual by collective values. Once recognized, apparently irreconcilable conflicts cease to afflict and distress us; rather, they become paths for learning, about ourselves and about others. They become more transparent, more ordinary, more useful.

The Changing Lines

This hexagram represents a time of dislocation and estrangement. With the exception of the first line, all the lines are in disagreement with their position (that is, yin lines in yang positions and vice versa) and this misfit between the two seems to reflect a strong experience of not knowing where one belongs, or with whom, or what to do about it.

9/1st   Our first instinct, when we experience the discomfort of discord or difference, is generally to try to fix it somehow. We chase after details under the illusion that if only we tweak the right one in the right way things will be fine. Instead, we might experiment with staying still with our confusion or anxiety and accepting deeply what is in the present moment. As disorderly or frightening as it may feel, by yielding to the energies at play we create a space in which a different ordering of those energies can emerge naturally because we are no longer resisting the situation.

9/2nd   Life will always confront us with the fact of opposites. No matter how wise or determined we become, any temporary reconciliation will always be followed by a new situation in which the play of opposition is experienced anew. Again and again we will need first to accept this as a universal truth of conditioned existence and then accept it in its immediate form in the present moment. Often the situation will then either resolve itself into a new balance or the required action will become clear and we can act confidently and decisively.

6/3rd   As time passes and a situation of discord persists, it is easy to become discouraged and feel impotent, torn by conflicting impulses and possibly baffled or enraged by recommendations from others. To call this suffering is not an exaggeration. The only way out is through it, one step at a time. Accepting our ignorance and confusion without judgement will lighten our load, as will recognizing that the outcome of any situation in life is rarely in our hands anyway.

9/4th   Opposition, or a 'siege' mentality, can lead to a blind survival mechanism taking over, at which point nothing creative can happen. Something has to 'give', and if we can initiate the giving by releasing some small thing (an attitude that has hardened, a version of events that places the blame elsewhere), then energies will be freed to flow again. In fact, it may be that we need to open up and receive something first, suggesting that issues of pride and humility may be evoked by the present situation.

6/5th   Fire and water, pictured in this hexagram as opposed to one another, cannot be considered as competitors; their natures are fundamentally different. At times we may become confused if we fail to recognize this distinction and persist in seeking a 'winner' and a 'loser'. Throughout life we may find ourselves in similar situations and, on account of misguidedly experiencing others as rivals rather than fellow travellers, we may lose the opportunity to learn from them and to share what we have learnt with them.

9/top   As the situation pictured in the hexagram draws to a close, we might hope to see reconciliation or acceptance of difference. Instead, in this case, we find hardness, contraction, perhaps a clinging to a view of events that perpetuates opposition but forecloses on learning and blocks healing. When we are identified with our opinion it is difficult to let go, even at the end. If we can manage it and allow a greater pattern to unfold, one that embraces the opposition that has been proving so troublesome, our experience of ourselves and the world we live in may undergo a transformation.

39. Chien / Obstruction

Primary Trigrams

above *K'an* / The Abysmal, Water
below *Kên* / Keeping Still, Mountain

Nuclear Trigrams

above *Li* / The Clinging, Fire
below *K'an* / The Abysmal, Water

The Mountain and the Abyss: these are the obstructions confronting us at this time. In addition, the image of water on the mountain reminds us of the way cloud and mist can shroud high peaks, lifting or dropping without warning, giving us a brief glimpse of the path or our location and then plunging us again into a world of vapour and illusion. We must watch our footing, keep our centre of gravity low, close to the ground. The mountain and the abyss represent substantial challenges or hurdles; they are neither imaginary nor superficial. None the less, they are also to be expected, as much a part of life here and now as they have been throughout the millennia of human development. Although within this situation the seeds of a future order lie ready, the way forward is not clear, and it is not a time to rush forward recklessly. There is an indication of danger both without and within; the former perhaps more easily identified than the latter. It is time to pause, to seek a deeper understanding of the situation, to turn inwards, accepting that the next part of the journey needs to be personal. It is difficult to be still and wait for the right moment when one's heart is pounding, but that is what is required now.

Every journey is a pilgrimage of sorts, the experience, challenges and meaning of which will be personal and individual. None the less, seeking guidance or fellowship before setting off is almost always a good idea, not as a substitute for reflection, but in recognition that the task is great and there is much to learn and others may have already passed this way or be willing to offer their love and support. As in *The Lord of the Rings*, fellowship can greatly strengthen the resources and resolve one needs to carry on with the task, even when, ultimately, each 'ring-bearer' must accomplish her task alone.

The Changing Lines

6/1st Faced with a 'mountain' and, beyond it, the unknown, this is the moment to pause, to gather oneself, to recognize a new chapter about to begin, to breathe out before breathing in. It is not the moment to fill one's mind with great ideas or pump up one's resolve. This moment will also mark the end of the previous chapter and attention might need to be paid to careful closure of what has gone before.

6/2nd Our own valuation of our abilities can present an obstacle. An over-valuation will probably be corrected fairly quickly, but an under-valuation may be more difficult. Feeling we are not up to a particular task physically or emotionally, not dynamic enough, can undermine our efforts before we even begin. We should seek others who will support us; not take over the job, but offer encouragement when we need it, advice if we seek it. We should also recognize that, however important this work is, we are just one link in a chain that stretches forward as far as it extends back into the past. We have our part to play but we need not feel responsible for the success or failure of the entire enterprise. If we do what has been given to us to do as well as we possibly can, that is enough.

9/3rd Once we have committed ourselves to the task or taken on the challenge presented by the times, we may grow impatient if results are not realized quickly. The temptation might be to forge ahead and leave others to clear up the details. Personal drives or desires can threaten to overwhelm the sense of a shared undertaking that can only thrive when each person is allowed to contribute out of their own gifts. This is a time for fellowship; out of that experience the next move will become clear.

6/4th   Not infrequently, obstacles present themselves when we least expect or welcome them. The idea that major events come in threes reflects this experience. The challenge is to find a point of balance that honours the energies and demands of the time but that allows us to wait before we take a decision. In the midst of conflicting claims we must seek to discern the creative decision from the expedient one.

9/5th   In the imagery of *The Lord of the Rings*, this figure is the Ring-Bearer. The weight of responsibility more or less consciously shouldered by this figure is tremendous. When we find ourselves in this position we need to cling to the adage, 'You have all that you need and you will need all that you have'. But we also need to be wary of self-importance, or the heroic attitude that can inflate and neutralize the quiet, courageous work of perseverance.

6/top   Our character is probably shaped to a greater extent by the difficult conditions and obstacles that we encounter in life than by the times of ease. The hardiest tree has experienced the nurture of sun and soil, but it will have also been tested and strengthened by extremes of weather. Freedom is won when we are open to whatever comes our way, when we no longer fear the 'storms' or desire perpetual pleasantness.

40. Hsieh / Deliverance

Primary Trigrams

above *Chên* / The Arousing, Thunder
below *K'an* / The Abysmal, Water

Nuclear Trigrams

above *K'an* / The Abysmal, Water
below *Li* / The Penetrating, Fire

The danger represented by lower primary trigram *K'an* has passed
(*K'an*'s natural movement is to sink) and new growth – *Chên* –
has already started (*Chên*'s natural movement is to rise). After a
thunderstorm, sometimes one can hear the rumbles of thunder as
they recede further and further into the distance while all around
the world seems new and clean; the air is cleared, the tension that
always builds in the atmosphere before a storm has been broken
or dissipated. In the situation pictured here, the storm has not
come suddenly but is, rather, the result of a build-up of factors. In
life there are often situations in which many contributing factors
can be seen, their history tracked, as they come together finally into
a moment of crisis that clears the air but might leave some wreck-
age in its wake. The earlier we are able to recognize the signs of
such a looming 'storm', the less destructive will it be. If we fail to
read such signs, not wishing to recognize the gathering danger,
we may wish afterwards that we had been more attentive or
courageous.

Following a storm, there may be salvage work to be done; we
may be a bit bruised or bewildered. It is important to understand
what has happened before moving on into the new beginning,
otherwise it may happen again. *Li* symbolizes this need for clear-
eyed understanding and enlightenment, while *K'an* indicates that
although the storm has passed there remains work to be done.

('[God] toils in the sign of the Abysmal', as the words of the *Shuo Kua* remind us.) The promise of a fresh start is not to be exploited, but rather accepted gratefully and with a commitment to sow new seeds with care and thoughtfulness, having, perhaps, reappraised our goals and priorities. There may also be some business from the past that should now be laid to rest; it is a time for forgiveness, amnesty, which is a sort of chosen forgetting.

The word, 'deliverance' has an almost Biblical ring to it. It is defined as 'rescue; salvation', which echoes the sense of (possibly, almost) divine intervention. A dangerous moment has passed, dividing time into 'before' and 'after'. It is appropriate to pause at such a moment, naming and acknowledging the significance of what has happened, experiencing our relief, or gratitude, or sadness before moving on.

The Changing Lines

After the storm has passed there may be a great urge to act, with the energy that was contracted in a sort of 'breath-holding' being suddenly released. The changing lines reflect this impulse to move, but in every case there should be a period of reflection of one sort or another first.

6/1st   The work of recovery starts here, and our first act should perhaps be some gesture of gratitude for our freedom from the threat that had been building to a climax. The narrating of a serious event can help to give it a context, to place it in the larger 'story' of our lives, to review and articulate its possible meanings or lessons. If we just rush on we miss this important opportunity for re-collecting ourselves.

9/2nd   The energy released by the 'storm' may be powerful and is, temporarily at least, unbound. If we feel charged up by events but have no way of channelling this energy, we can easily find ourselves attracted to the person or idea that appears to offer a comparable 'high'. Coming down to earth is very important, finding pleasure in small things, resuming our ordinary patterns of life. This is not the same as purposely seeking a risk-free or compromised existence; it is about simply grounding our energies.

6/3rd More often than not, it is within relationships that the dynamics addressed by this hexagram occur. There we must continually negotiate the balances between individual needs and goals and the requirements of a fruitful partnership. Fluctuations in feelings are part of the rhythm of any relationship, and conflicts may develop apparently out of nowhere. At times these may take on the character of a crisis. To understand the elements that have brought us to this point and to discern their true nature may require patience, but it will provide a sort of deliverance in itself.

9/4th On the one hand, it is rare in life to be offered a fresh start, a blank slate on which to write a new story; on the other hand, moment by moment we can pause and seek new and fresh responses to the events of life. We have resources within that we may never tap, of which we may be completely ignorant. If we are offered the opportunity of a new beginning, we do well to take the time to commit ourselves to going forward mindfully and with curiosity, rather than allowing ourselves to be simply propelled into the next instalment of our life story.

6/5th When we feel battered by the sheer ongoingness of the demands and challenges of life, it is hard even to imagine a time when things might flow more easily, when we might again feel able to rest and to recover our balance. If, in addition, we struggle against such testing times, telling ourselves that they are somehow 'wrong', we only increase the burden. These times are exceptional; if they persist without change or relief then we probably need to pause and consider if there might be an entirely different way of looking at the situation. Discussing it honestly with others who care for us and are capable of insight might also help. Life is a process that is constantly changing; if it is blocked, for whatever reason, we should place ourselves at the point of blockage and open ourselves to deliverance.

6/top When we sense that a situation is on the cusp of change we may feel a degree of anxiety about our role in that process: do we press for the change to happen – tip the scales in that direction – or do we wait and see? There is a way of attending on events that involves a combination of readiness, clear-sightedness, and trust. When we begin to see a new pattern or rhythm or energy emerging, we are then able to join it at the 'right' moment, a moment that is natural and congruent.

41. Sun / Decrease

Primary Trigrams

above *Kên* / Keeping Still, Mountain
below *Tui* / The Joyous, Lake

Nuclear Trigrams

above *K'un* / The Receptive, Earth
below *Chên* / The Arousing Water

This hexagram is considered to have evolved from *T'ai* / Peace, in that the lower primary trigram *Ch'ien* of the latter has willingly decreased its strength by giving up one of its strong lines to the upper primary trigram *K'un*. The resulting hexagram pictures a lake at the foot of the mountain, an image that also contains the idea of exchange, as the moisture from the lake rises and benefits the vegetation on the mountain.

While balance is a central ideal in the *I Ching*, it is always dynamic, never static, and this hexagram takes this idea to a deeper level. The 'mandala' of Taoism presents us with a circle in which a black tadpole-like form spirals around – and is spiralled around by – a white tadpole-like form. Each also contains an 'eye' within of the other colour, black in white and white in black. This familiar motif demonstrates the principle of dynamic balance, showing us that fullness and emptiness is a constantly varying exchange between the yin and the yang. As with a see-saw, where balance is achieved and movement is maintained between the rising side and the falling side through the active and constant adjustment of weight by the individuals on either end, so there are times when we must adjust, lightening something in one place in order that more might be carried in another. In this case, the adjustment is made by relinquishing some of the strength 'below' in favour of an increase in strength 'above'. As the lower primary trigram is more representative of the earth and of material existence and the upper primary trigram of the philosophical or spiritual, this is an exchange that seems to require some sacrifice on the material level, and to make such a choice can often be difficult, if not painful. The counsel at such a time is to simplify one's life, to be mindful of expenditure of all sorts, financial, physical, emotional, to cultivate stillness and sincerity, to review priorities and realign ourselves with that which we consider most profoundly truthful within. Western culture encourages us to 'go for it all', as if only the principle of growth was operating and not also that of decay and change. To participate in the process by evaluating what might be sacrificed in our lives in the interests of enhancing other aspects of our lives is to align ourselves with the Tao of the universe and helps in making something meaningful of the decrease, the self-denial.

At such a time, the creation of a private ritual may be very helpful in that it creates a symbolic space in which we honour our choice to let go, at the same time witnessing to our belief in the possibility of transformation through this decrease. Even something as simple as consulting the *I Ching* brings us into the present moment, heightening self-awareness and supporting our intention to learn and grow.

Finally, a further emphasis is on the decrease and softening of anger or anything that has become hard and fixed, opinions, versions of events, visions of the future. As in the mandala of Taoism described above, everything in the conditional world contains the seed of its opposite within. We must allow seeds of doubt to co-exist with even our most cherished ideas.

The Changing Lines

The principle of decrease or exchange, as described above, can occur either within the individual or between individuals, when one person chooses to relinquish something, perhaps power, in favour of another person. In this latter case, all the comments below also apply, but perhaps one needs to be even more careful in understanding why the choice to do so is being made and what reward one might have in mind. True altruism or generosity is a wonderful quality, but it is often tinged with other motives.

9/1st The circumstances pictured by the hexagram are in their early stages, and there is no better time to lighten our load than at the start of a journey. The sort of 'baggage' we might be carrying could be a desire for a particular outcome, or a definite view of how the journey should go, or how we should feel, or the idea that we should accomplish this undertaking on our own, unaided. Such attitudes weigh us down at every turn and blind us to the unexpected. The more willing we are to let go, the readier we will be for whatever learning and adventure lie ahead. The transfer of energy here is from an anxious investment in an old balance that worked to the possibility of a new balance emerging out of the process of change and challenge to which we are committing ourselves.

9/2nd The challenges inherent in the concept of sacrifice are great; we can easily slip into an expectation of reward, or into masochistic denial, or into a regressed dependence on others. At all times we are responsible for ourselves and our priorities. Decrease and increase are two sides of one coin and they will both be reflected in our inner experience. It may help if we ask ourselves honestly in what way we have gained – or hope to gain – by choosing to give something up.

6/3rd The 'fulcrum' of the hexagram and the present situation lies here; this is the interface where the exchange, the shift, takes place. We should take root in this moment, recognizing its importance and enjoying its promise without feeling we are personally responsible for the realization of its potential. Our part is simply to let go willingly.

6/4th The time after an exchange has taken place or a sacrifice has been made can be trying. We want a result; we want confusion to resolve itself; we want to feel better, and we may feel nothing; we may feel worse. Instinctively, but prematurely, we may seek to clarify what has happened, to sum it up into something knowable from which we can move on. Instead, we must learn to tolerate our discomfort and the untidiness of the times.

6/5th When decrease and increase are understood not so much as reciprocal processes but as a unified flow in which it is impossible to differentiate one from the other, then we are seeing through the imperfections of language to a greater reality. We may glimpse this from time to time but, in general, we must live with the familiar duality. Opening and softening ourselves to those others with whom we share this particular moment creates an environment in which all may be enriched.

9/top   Within the world of the hexagram, this position represents the individual who benefited from the original decrease, the sacrifice made by others. Now this individual, in turn, is asked to accept his own diminishment and make way for new growth and increase. Of course, this is a statement about the rhythm of life itself.

42. I / Increase

Primary Trigrams

above *Sun* / The Gentle, Wood, Wind
below *Chên* / The Arousing, Thunder

Nuclear Trigrams

above *K'an* / The Abysmal, Water
below *K'un* / The Receptive, Earth

This hexagram represents a development of *Pi* / Standstill (hexagram 12). In the latter, the three yielding lines of *K'un* (lower primary trigram) sink into the earth while the three firm lines of *Ch'ien* (upper primary trigram) rise up to heaven. The situation reflected in that hexagram is one in which there is no mutual benefit to be gained; one 'party' goes in one direction and the other goes in the opposite. There is no sense of shared vision or common resources, no overlap. Without engagement and relationship, a situation becomes stagnant or disintegrates; there is no way forward. The resolution pictured in the present hexagram shows us that there has been an exchange: Heaven has given a firm line to Earth and received a yielding line from Earth, thus creating the dynamic and fruitful engagement of *Chên*, the Arousing, the initiating, and *Sun*, the Gentle, the Penetrating. An intercourse has taken place where before there was only increasing distance, and there is a suggestion that this has come about through recognizing that individual gifts, if shared rather than hoarded, can become tools that benefit all and open the way for further creative development.

There is a particular quality to the good times that come about through the recognition that 'less is more', a sense that we have all learned something and gained from the experience, a feeling of celebration that the 'right' choices were made for the 'right' reasons. This is generativity in action, and it demonstrates how practical and sensible it is to release and share. Not only does it show that it is safe to do so, but it also encourages others to do the same. The transformation from Standstill to Increase, which is the dynamic illustrated by *I*, is not a one-way gift; both Heaven, The Creative, and Earth, The Receptive, give and receive.

This is a pragmatic hexagram: giving and receiving are chosen not for altruistic reasons or out of simple goodness of heart, but rather because that is what works. When one knows what works the choice is easy.

The Changing Lines

9/1st Within the terms of the hexagram, this is the position that has benefited from the exchange. The way is clear and we should now be able to move forward with resolution and the promise of 'success'. But sometimes it is not until we find ourselves in this position that we realize whatever was formerly preventing movement, that which has now been rectified, was not the whole story. We find we are still hesitant. We need to devote every effort to understanding and clarifying our thoughts and feelings, perhaps consulting with others, listening to different views, being prepared to learn wholly new truths.

6/2nd When we are able to receive without feeling diminished, everybody benefits and the conditions for increase are expanded. We should not indulge in needless or craven expressions of gratitude or unworthiness; giving and receiving constitute the rhythm of the breath of life. Our responsibility is to remain open and prepared to release the good that has come our way whenever and wherever this is required; to become, ourselves, the giver.

6/3rd Here, in the middle of the hexagram, lies the interface between the giver and the receiver, and it reflects a position we may find ourselves in when we feel hungry for something and measure the size of what we imagine we need against this hunger. In fact, it may be that what we most need is some sort of affirmation that we have all we need to go forward already, that our strengths are sufficient to move out of and away from our present position of safety. En-courage-ment.

6/4th   Some people seem to be able to serve as a channel for the movement of energy to wherever it is most needed. They neither block this flow nor divert it for their own needs. If we experience life as fundamentally abundant, then serving the common good in this way will happen naturally. If, on the other hand, we feel there is not enough to go around, we will be inclined to grab and hoard. Fear makes the difference.

9/5th   This position is considered to carry with it recognition and a degree of responsibility. Within the terms of the hexagram it represents an individual who is attentive to the needs of others, not in a superficial way that offers immediate but insubstantial satisfaction, but in a way that leads to true increase. This is an important distinction and one that applies equally in the intrapersonal sphere.

9/top   If we hold on too tightly to the good things in life, we interrupt the flow of energy that moves between increase and decrease in an eternal rhythm. In fact, in spite of holding on we may lose what we have, because, in contracting around present fears about loss, we effectively squeeze the life out of that which we value. When the situation changes we may find our 'treasure' is no longer useful. If we recognize our difficulty in letting go and sharing, and direct compassion towards ourselves and our helplessness, we might at least increase our capacity for tenderness where it most matters.

43. Kuai / Breakthrough (Resoluteness)

Primary Trigrams

above *Tui* / The Joyous, Lake
below *Ch'ien* / The Creative, Heaven

Nuclear Trigrams

above *Ch'ien* / The Creative, Heaven
below *Ch'ien* / The Creative, Heaven

The single 'dark' or yielding line at the top of *Kuai* gives rise to a number of different interpretations of this hexagram. The first association draws upon the imagery of rain/water (*Tui*) in heaven (*Ch'ien*). A storm threatens; the atmosphere bristles with accumulated tension that will only be released once the clouds release their burden. This interpretation addresses those times when we are faced with situations in which escalating tension must be addressed lest it run the risk of becoming dangerous. If we neglect to defuse such situations they may re-balance themselves in a dramatic, even frightening, way. The equalizing tendency of nature means that sooner or later an accumulation in one place will be dispersed or redistributed, violently, as in earthquakes, or more gradually, as in the slow erosion of mountains. In human affairs we do well to regularly consider what may be excessive accumulation, because anything, if it is stored up for too long, risks a dramatic levelling off.

Another strand of interpretation that is reflected in the presence of the solitary yin line at the top of the hexagram concerns the danger of what Jung called 'Shadow' elements within ourselves, between us and others, or in politics or institutional life. All human beings suffer from feelings of envy and greed. It is in our nature to compare ourselves with others in the endless pursuit of self-esteem and we can always find somebody who seems 'luckier', better endowed, better supported, happier, more successful. All our unacceptable feelings become part of our personal shadow, an aspect of ourselves that we dislike and disapprove of and, if possible, deny. We generally find we are particularly hostile to people who we feel exhibit exactly those faults that we dislike and have denied in ourselves. These may well be the people with whom we experience the greatest conflict, and so it is very much in our interest to understand the dynamics whereby we experience in others what is actually our own. This requires great determination, however, and a willingness to recognize the 'beam' in our own eye before we accuse others of a 'mote' in theirs. Once it is possible to face oneself honestly, it becomes much easier to deal with conflict. The single yin line at the top of the hexagram represents something apparently small but, none the less, important that must be dealt with, something 'dark' that is blocking the full 'light'. It is surprising how often we imagine that the problem lies outside ourselves when, in fact, we are allowing a compromising situation to continue because there is some small element in it to which it suits us to turn a blind eye. We continue to profit from it in a shadowy way.

Finally, the open line at the top represents the mouth. In all that has been said above, the importance of addressing complex issues presupposes a considerable degree of consciousness and, consequently, the constructive and creative use of language. If we deal with conflict and difficulty in a primitive, non-verbal way, the cycle of build-up–blow-up–build-up simply perpetuates itself indefinitely. Once we are capable of thinking about an issue, describing and discussing it with others or reflecting on it by ourselves, a way forward exists. If we wish to achieve what all would recognize as a breakthrough, there must be resoluteness (the alternative name for this hexagram), openness, and a real desire to understand and de-escalate the situation.

This is a calendar hexagram representing the fourth month of the Chinese calendar, April–May.

The Changing Lines

9/1st   If resoluteness is called for, every moment of delay will only increase the urgency of the situation. It is also in our interests to act sooner rather than later, as delay tends to weaken resolve. It is only necessary to take the first step with courage and conviction; we do not have to solve all problems at once.

9/2nd If we can clear our minds and see things as they really are, elements that have been indistinct or shadowy will be revealed and we will recognize what must be addressed; however, if we deny the truth about a situation and allow ourselves to be taken by surprise, it can be devastating. Fear has no place at such a time and no hold over the person who is prepared.

9/3rd Within the context of the hexagram, this position lies at a crucial point in the process of breakthrough, a point when resolve may be tested and where we may need to dig deeper to find an extra degree of courage or vision. It is not a time for idle or careless behaviour; nor should we allow ourselves to become rough, impatient, or anxious. A light touch and a steady mind will serve us best.

9/4th Sometimes we will find ourselves in a situation where we simply must accept a period of waiting and uncertainty before we will be able to effect the resolution that we desire. While we wait we should consider deeply all the ways in which this situation is affecting us and be ruthlessly honest with ourselves. If we fail in this task it will be almost impossible for us to recognize the way through when it appears.

9/5th This line represents a person of integrity and resolution. He is faced with a situation in which, paradoxically, advance can only be achieved by an apparent retreat. Whatever the actual issues are, it is through recognition of the tremendous temptations of the exercise of power and its capacity to corrupt that this person finds his true strength. True greatness can be measured by its readiness to acknowledge weakness. This is an example of the strange affinity between the darkest and the lightest elements of human nature: they are connected through the shadow, and if light can be cast on that darkness, previously bound energy is released and becomes available.

6/top When, through resolute action, the small but vital element that has been blocking progress is removed, we must not deceive ourselves that this is an accomplished fact, for once and for all. In fact, this yin line will reappear: after the month of greatest light (May–June, represented by the hexagram Ch'ien), the dark re-enters (see the following hexagram Kou / Coming to Meet). Similarly, we never rid the world altogether of the Shadow: we name it, address it, both within and without, learn about its powers, integrate our new wisdom or experience and then carry on, knowing that it will appear again, that it must appear again, and that it is through such resolute work when it does appear that we have the opportunity to learn and grow.

44. Kou / Coming To Meet

Primary Trigrams

above *Ch'ien* / The Creative, Heaven
below *Sun* / The Gentle, Wind, Wood

Nuclear Trigrams

above *Ch'ien* / The Creative, Heaven
below *Ch'ien* / The Creative, Heaven

The summer solstice has just passed, the brightest day of the year, and now, at the beginning of the fifth month in the Chinese calendar, June–July, the dark enters again from the bottom of the hexagram. This trend will continue until November–December, when the hexagram *K'un*, standing for the tenth month, receives a yang line at the bottom, beginning the cycle of the seasons again at the winter solstice. This is the course of nature, for us as well as for the annual rhythms. Were it not for the process of decay, new birth could not take place. Last year's leaves and fallen branches and fallen bodies provide the growing medium for next year's fruits and flowers. Death – here represented by the dark line in the first position – enters boldly and unafraid and faces the light as an equal principle, if not yet an equal force.

Although the natural cycle of the seasons is recognized in the *I Ching*, in this particular hexagram the re-entry of the dark is seen as dangerous and something to be dealt with quickly, before it grows into a more serious threat. This interpretation emphasizes the importance of recognizing and containing the earliest signs of negative or 'Shadow' elements. It counsels that the apparently weak, small, and unobtrusive entry of the feminine or dark principle must not be underestimated or entertained under the misguided notion that it is not very important. The 'thin end of the wedge' is the easiest part to insert into a narrow crack, but driven in bit by bit, it finally achieves the goal of splitting the wood. We need to be vigilant with ourselves as well as socially or politically, guarding against complacency in the face of a small, but clearly subversive element that we detect. Pretending it doesn't matter or that it will go away is not the solution.

It is interesting to note the difference in tone between the commentaries on this present hexagram and on Number 24, *Fu / Return*. The return of the light is an event to be welcomed and celebrated, and the new growth is to be tended with care; the return of the dark is viewed as a dangerous time. It is understandable that we fear the cold, unproductive, and dark winter (we are at our most vulnerable then), but our culture has done nothing to moderate those fears of the unknown and 'dark' elements. We need more than ever to learn to acknowledge and own the dark to be as much a part of our lives and our characters as the light. Jung repeated this over and over again: if we do not make this effort to deal with the dark as an intimate part of ourselves we will end up projecting it on to others, other religions, other people, and then we will do battle with it externally, and learn nothing. Dealing with the dark has many ramifications, and the first encounter of the light and the dark, reflected in this hexagram, is an important time.

On a more general note, while the associations to the feminine or yin principle often seem negative, it is important to recognize the fundamental play and interaction of the complementary principles of yin and yang, masculine and feminine, firm and yielding, light and dark, without assigning value to one or the other. In this hexagram, the progress of the light has passed the point of its greatest magnitude and, naturally, the dark will now gain ascendancy until it reaches its extreme. However, the mistrust of the feminine principle continues and is legendary. It will always pose a threat to clarity and rationality because it moves in another element. It represents the dark of the earth and the womb, the mysteries of sexuality and death. There is no better example of this principle than Kali, the terrifyingly beautiful and powerful Hindu deity who has been allowed to retain the whole spectrum of creativity and destruction. Were we more able to acknowledge and celebrate the 'Kali' part of ourselves – and of life – we would be less likely to fear and fall victim to her, without or within.

The Changing Lines

6/1st   This line represents the new element that the commentary on the hexagram addresses. We may react to the new or the different with curiosity and openness or with a contraction that, in itself, creates a barrier and turns the clock back. In addition, it may force this element to go 'underground', and there it could gain strength, which might not be a good idea if it represents a real danger. If we ourselves identify with this 'different' element as we approach a difficult or challenging situation, the counsel would be the same, to remain quietly alert, open, and curious and not to run for cover if we are met with suspicion.

9/2nd   The situation represented by this hexagram does not allow us to do nothing; that is not an option. However, it is not an admission of defeat if we adapt to the new circumstances by becoming still and thoughtful, acknowledging the reality of what is happening but choosing not to struggle against it. In this way we do nothing to prevent the flow of the times, but neither do we join it willy-nilly.

9/3rd   Events may have already moved on before we become aware of what has happened and we may be called upon to do something. Rarely does the *I Ching* counsel impulsive action and here is no different; this choice would probably only lead to further divisiveness rather than engagement. On the other hand, sometimes matters are already so bad that acting instinctively clarifies that which has become obscured by unsatisfactory compromises. It is a risky strategy; it would be better to take time to clarify one's own thoughts and feelings before resorting to more dramatic measures that may achieve nothing.

9/4th   The intention behind our deeds is as important as the deeds themselves. If we approach an uncertain situation with the intention of finding a way forward that truly benefits all concerned and a willingness to learn from and about the new circumstances, then we cannot go far wrong, as long as we are not being disingenuous about a real danger.

9/5th   In the position that generally represents the ideal response to a situation we find a combination of strength and creativity. There is an indication of how this is achieved, and that is through a profound identification with the new, 'dark' element through which we and the element itself are transformed. This accords with the idea that the entry of the dark or death line is not something that need be feared; if it can be encompassed and included as one of the infinite number of faces of Life, then it becomes a resource rather than a threat.

9/top   The motivation behind deciding to align ourselves with an unknown, possibly subversive, possibly simply different energy at the last possible moment should always be examined, particularly in the light of how this choice will affect others. That the decision was made out of ignorance is not an acceptable defence.

45. Ts'ui / Gathering Together

Primary Trigrams

above *Tui* / The Joyous, Lake
below *K'un* / The Receptive, Earth

Nuclear Trigrams

above *Sun* / The Gentle, Wind, Wood
below *Kên* / Keeping Still, Mountain

The waters of the earth are gathered together in a lake. This hexagram addresses the situation where individuals – or individual aspects of one person – are drawn together more or less intentionally. This hexagram differs from *Pi* / Holding Together (Hexagram 8) in that the latter concerns the general flowing together of all the waters of the earth as they move towards the seas and oceans. Implied in that image is the force of affinity, like drawing like. Here the emphasis lies more in examining the nature of chosen congregations, how they are managed, what or who acts as a strong enough attraction for others. In terms of the individual herself becoming more 'gathered', we might enquire as to how we become coherent human beings, with a core experience of ourselves, able to make balanced decisions and exercise wise judgement. Without this central core, our energies are so dispersed and dissipated that we can no longer act in a coherent manner.

One question we might ask in such a situation is, 'Where have I come from?' Having a sense of origin can provide stability, whether it is geographical, tribal, philosophical, or simply family. We might ask this of somebody who wants to draw us to himself or his cause. The question, 'Where has he come from?' then equates to understanding what the nature of his motivation might be, and this might help us to clarify our own choice. There is a time for allowing dreams and imagination to have full play, but this is not such a time. Now we need to be well anchored in reality, the reality of Here and Now. It is a time in which we are called to 're-member' ourselves, re-collect ourselves, re-create ourselves. This work requires commitment and perseverance as well as a capacity to stand back and reflect on questions of who and why and how rather than acting impulsively or instinctually.

In general, when we are drawn to a gathering or a joint undertaking, we should consider whether something lasting is likely to be the outcome, something of value. Are we really prepared to contribute wholeheartedly? Are we really in agreement with the aims? Have we been dangerously disarmed by the arguments of one person or another? Or, we might need to consider if we ourselves should be thinking about taking on a leadership role. These questions require a quiet heart and mind, the state of being gathered or 'collected', the word chosen by Prospero in *The Tempest* when he counsels his daughter Miranda to calm herself and regain control of her mind and emotions.

The Changing Lines

6/1st   This hexagram suggests a time of rebalancing, of making conscious our goals and possibly repositioning ourselves in relation to others. The effort involved will require concentration, maturity, and a willingness to act and choose decisively, not impulsively, but with intent and energy. We should try to remove our 'blinkers' and may need others to help us identify our blind spots.

6/2nd   If we have never questioned our goals and alliances before, it may be difficult to know where to start, especially if we have been followers rather than leaders. While the task is an important one, even an essential one, we should try not to take it so seriously that we lose touch with others and, in particular, with our ordinary human limitations. The journey of increasing awareness is a life-long one; there is no need to rush it or take on more than we are able to cope with at any given time.

6/3rd   In the thick of our searching or questioning, our efforts to become a coherent individual, we may lose our sense of what it is we want from others, or from the 'outside' world.

This confusion may render us quite vulnerable to those who are looking for a congregation and we should take care not to align ourselves prematurely with exciting ideas or movements. Simply and quietly persevering with our 'work' is enough for the time being.

9/4th   The character and qualities of a facilitator are sometimes relegated to an inferior position compared to those of a leader, yet this position requires tact, intuition, and a capacity to balance and moderate the needs of the times and all involved. The challenge for such a person is in continuing to limit himself to just pointing the way, and this self-limitation itself should be frequently re-examined.

9/5th   Leadership must always be based on the dynamic of listening to and honing our own judgement with as much honesty as possible while also listening, with equal attention and honesty, to the voices of others. There is a Buddhist saying, 'Of the two witnesses, hold the principal one'. This means we should be truly open to the views of others but, in the end, we must work with our own view, our own truth, and take responsibility for the consequences of our choices.

6/top   Although the balance differs in each of us, we are all both social and solitary creatures, and we move back and forth between these two ways of being throughout life. The more self-aware we are, the more likely it is that we will seek either company or solitude when we become aware that we need it rather than waiting until the last moment and either bolting without explanation or jumping unwisely into whatever group presents itself first.

46. Shêng / Pushing Upward

Primary Trigrams

above *K'un* / The Receptive, Earth
below *Sun* / The Gentle, The Penetrating, Wind, Wood

Nuclear Trigrams

above *Chên* / The Arousing, Thunder
below *Tui* / The Joyous, Lake

Sun, representing wood or a new shoot, lies beneath *K'un*, Earth, and is pushing its way upwards. The presence of *Chên*, the trigram of spring, suggests that the seedling will be well supported and nurtured. The growing shoot adapts to obstacles and to exposure and continues to rise, bending and growing without haste. This hexagram shows us clearly the natural energy and impulse of life. As surely as spring follows winter, the tremendous vitality and regenerative capacity of life ensures that new growth will appear and flourish wherever and whenever conditions allow.

In human life, too, new growth occurs whenever and wherever it is encouraged and supported. Unfortunately, we often hold back such encouragement out of fear or mistrust, and our hesitation and lack of wholeheartedness mean we put only a portion of our energy into furthering new growth. If a seedling were as reserved in its effort, it would quickly lose out to others with greater determination. The hexagram counsels us not only to have more faith in the process of growth and creativity, but also to invest real energy in it. We use the phrase, 'fence-sitting' to describe times when we are not committing ourselves to one course or another, waiting to see how things develop. This is not a time for diffidence; on the contrary, it would be wasteful to turn away from an opportunity that is both supported by the times and also imbued with real potential. We rarely know the outcome in advance, whether a particular idea or project or path will prosper, but it stands a greater chance of doing so if we put ourselves wholly behind it.

In spite of all that has been said, having committed oneself to the energy of life and growth, a certain sadness or regret about what has been left behind may well be experienced. The roads not taken can seem, retrospectively, to have held out more promise. Life moves on and there is no way back. Such sadness is natural and need not lead to bitterness. Not all things are possible: this is what it means to be mortal. The *I Ching* gives us pointers as to how to surmount obstacles and continue to grow in personal character and wisdom. It is very pragmatic and does not dwell long on sadness or the more bitter experience of regret. Yet these are familiar feelings for us all, and it is as important that we recognize them and their reference points as that we recognize other indicators of the times.

The Changing Lines

6/1st Growth begins within the earth. It is here that the first roots must establish and nourish themselves. It is the same for us: we must first find a place to embed and send out the 'shoots' that will be our anchors and channels for nourishment. Only then can we move beyond survival to growth. So strong is the instinct for life that it is almost inextinguishable, given even the bleakest of conditions. We should never underestimate the importance of remaining 'earthed' in our shared humanity; reaching out to others for support, guidance or simply for human warmth can transform a situation that might otherwise feel desolate.

9/2nd Sometimes the first step in a new direction is easier than the second. If we have envisioned great returns on our early resolution, we are likely to be disappointed and this could become the first real test of commitment. The input, advice, or support of others – inner or outer, friendly or otherwise – could play an important role in either helping or preventing us from moving on. At such a time it is probably wise to pause and reflect briefly, and then to take the next step without fanfare but with quiet determination. Pride itself can become an obstacle.

9/3rd   At a certain point we may experience a pull backwards that is almost as strong as the pull forwards. Whether it is regret for that which we have left behind, fearfulness about what lies ahead, or some residual issue or unresolved conflict that is acting as a 'drag' on us, this could be a challenging time. Ultimately, our future choices and judgement will be affected if we do not commit ourselves to bringing these issues to consciousness and addressing them. Once we have done so we may well feel a surge of vitality and hope.

6/4th   Conditions that favour rapid early growth may leave new shoots vulnerable when those conditions change, whereas harsh early conditions may so impede growth that the young plant finds itself forced out of the space it requires for growth by other, more opportunistically successful competitors. Life seems to alternate between challenge and encouragement and, as always, wisdom lies in the dynamic balance of yin and yang, in seizing the opportunity to advance when the time allows it and in accepting limitation when it is unavoidable. There is a Native American saying that applies here: 'The horse that carries the traveller on the journey of search for the gifts of the four directions is named Patience'.

6/5th   Throughout life, we grow through the alternating rhythms of self-discovery and 'tribal' identifications. Our view of ourselves will change as dramatically as our sense of where and to what group we belong. Each step builds on the last balance we achieved and every step of the process is essential; no part is too small or too apparently trivial not to be valuable. No matter how far we go on the path of personal growth, we must always be aware of our responsibility to return what we have learnt and gained for the common good, however we manage this. Brilliance is only an achievement if it helps to lighten the darkness, if it makes it possible for others to see.

6/top   Letting go is rarely easy, and the top line of a hexagram represents this challenge in relation to the particular circumstances of the times. On this threshold between the 'knowns' of the past and the unknowns of the future, we are best served by a quiet heart and a curious attitude. In

particular, we may need to honestly assess our recent experience and seek to clarify areas where we feel disappointed
or disheartened. There may be long-standing reasons for
our disappointment: perhaps no achievement has ever been
satisfying, yet we continue to seek some elusive sense of
completion. We should not be content with superficial
answers.

47. K'un / Oppression (Exhaustion)

Primary Trigrams

above *Tui* / The Joyous, Lake
below *K'an* / The Abysmal, Water

Nuclear Trigrams

above *Sun* / The Gentle, The Penetrating, Wind, Wood
below *Li* / The Clinging, Fire

This hexagram pictures an exceptional time when the waters of the
lake have either evaporated or been drained off into an underlying
abyss. The exhaustion of the waters happens in two ways, one a
more 'outer' way and the other a more 'inner' way. The first is
through evaporation, to the clouds; the second is through a loss that
occurs out of sight and 'beneath' the lake. In terms of an individual,
the difference is between a loss of vital energy through, in effect,
giving it away to the outside world, or other people, and a loss of
energy that is due to the activation of an inner 'black hole', a draining away of energy in the unconscious. In certain circumstances
these two may be connected, in that an inability to husband one's
resources and care for oneself rather than always prioritizing others
is not infrequently a reflection of a profound lack of self-esteem. It
is clear that the signals of feeling oppressed or exhausted must be
attended to without delay; if we continue, we risk a sort of physical, emotional, or spiritual bankruptcy or collapse, and all our
resources may become exhausted.

The individual who finds him or herself in this situation is
'between a rock and a hard place'. Such a time calls for – and
develops – a strong and enduring character. Unlike other hexagrams that involve waiting for the times to change (for instance
Hexagram 5, *Hsü* / Waiting, where we are advised to enjoy food
and drink and company while waiting for a change in conditions),

here the conditions must be addressed without delay because, in spite of the perception that the world is the problem, the real source of the problem resides in the individual. At such a time we should speak little and cultivate a quiet attitude with regard to the outer world and a curious one with regard to ourselves, being ready to affirm and explore our individual needs and unique way of being in the world. As a consequence of such reflection, we may need to make difficult decisions in order to be true to what we have discovered. A sense of relief and even lightness may accompany this process and a feeling that, after all, it is possible to envision a way through these testing times.

Another image that might be helpful in considering the relevance of this hexagram to the times is that of the iceberg, where only the smallest fraction of the whole is visible above water. Whatever portion of our lives is visible to others, or even to ourselves, the far greater portion lies out of sight, and the greater part of that is unknowable and inaccessible. We are the living link in a chain of human lives, choices, and experiences that reaches back into immeasurable time. We – and the times we live in – have been shaped by all those earlier lives, but each of us is also unique. At this time it may be helpful to think about how we view or work with this balance.

The Changing Lines

6/1st   Acknowledging exhaustion or identifying feelings of oppression is the first step in the process of recovery; indeed, at times, simply naming our feelings alters our experience of them. We then must find a way of 'sealing off' the point at which vital energy is draining away. We will only prolong the dysfunction if we attribute it to external factors; the loss is occurring deep within us at a point where we are vulnerable to fears and fantasies. Once brought to awareness, it is likely that we will find new ways of addressing these fears and they will no longer oppress us in the same way.

9/2nd   While every human being is unique, we are also ordinary, in that the fundamental events and processes of life apply equally – if not even-handedly – to us all. Sometimes we equate ordinariness with being boring, or we experience boredom in the face of the sheer ongoingness of daily life. This is not a superficial problem; it may reflect a deep sense of loss of meaning and purpose and, if not recognized and addressed, could lead to real despair and depression. The inclination to dismiss these conditions or not take them seriously works against the importance of committing oneself to the task of deep reflection and inner work. Our connection to others – past, present and future – can serve to ground and support us through difficult times, but if we cannot afford to see ourselves as anything other than 'special', it may make it hard for us to reach out.

6/3rd   From time to time most of us find ourselves simply carrying too much, trying to be everywhere at once. We must find a way of releasing something, letting something go, and this may prove a real challenge. We need to learn to expect less of ourselves, perhaps also of others. Expectations carry consequences when they are disappointed – feelings of rage, hurt, depression, futility – and, in seeking to avoid the discomfort of such consequences, we continue to load more and more on ourselves (and/or others). Eventually it becomes impossible for anything to work out and then it may all 'crash' around us. We must learn acceptance and forgiveness and, above all, stop fighting life.

9/4th   At times we may need to go in what would appear to be exactly the opposite direction from that which seems to be indicated. Rather than seeking to neutralize or escape from the conditions that are oppressive, we may be better served by moving deeply into them, offering no resistance and with an attitude of curiosity rather than fear. This choice is really about moving more deeply into our own nature, letting go of rigid control and allowing ourselves to 'flow' into life more. Everything that comes into life comes in wild; amazingly, we seem unaware of how readily we give away our wildness or what a treasure it is.

9/5th   When times are difficult and we are tired, we naturally try to 'pull ourselves together' in order to get through; we create a sort of protective shell because we feel vulnerable and we forge on. This is courageous and may work as long as it does not have to be sustained for too long; however, we may not learn much from managing to keep going in this way. A better way forward might be to simply accept that we are in a process and the immediate experience of that process is one of heaviness and fatigue. We do not always need to understand – leave alone remedy – the causes or dynamics of a situation. The first Noble Truth of Buddhism states that everything changes; this time of oppression will pass and, knowing that, we might finally be able to rest.

6/top The sixth position – the top of the hexagram – represents the closing stages of a situation. If, at this point, there has been no resolution, we should consider the possibility that at the heart of the ongoing struggle lie two fundamentally opposed principles or energies and that they are irreconcilable. Our ability to envision other possible outcomes has been limited by our exhaustion; we must step back from the struggle and allow these possibilities to emerge.

48. Ching / The Well

Primary Trigrams

above *K'an* / The Absymal, Water
below *Sun* / The Gentle, Wind, Wood

Nuclear Trigrams

above *Li* / The Clinging, Fire
below *Tui*, The Joyous, Lake

Below upper primary trigram *K'an*, signifying deep water, ground-water, we find *Sun*, signifying Wood. Right away the image presents us with a relationship: a resource and something that is drawing on that resource – here, the groundwater or spring and the wooden bucket (or it could be the roots of a plant). The image contains the message of this hexagram: without the well, the spring water would just trickle away; without the bucket the well water would be tantalizing but unattainable; without a rope (or a pole, in China) the bucket would be useless, and without a person at the top of the well lowering the bucket far enough to bring up the water, all the rest would be irrelevant. The final link, to extend the chain beyond the individual, might be the wider family or community, and at this point the individual becomes a 'well' herself. The union of all elements – in a person as in a well – is what allows the 'water' to be drawn and to reach those who need it.

It is easy to grasp the importance of the issues suggested by this image: the ever-bubbling water of the spring is Life or wisdom (or the Tao) and we construct the well in order to have it as a resource. The *I Ching* is one such 'well' and there are many others, but they are just the 'bricks and mortar' that we employ to contain a portion of that which is ultimately uncontainable. The bucket is the vessel we use to draw an even smaller portion up to nourish ourselves and others; it may be a symbol of consciousness, of intention, of desire. Similarly, the rope, a symbol of patience or endurance/ perseverance: do we provide enough 'rope' so that it can go all the way down to where the deep water lies, or do we lower it a bit and, finding nothing but air, draw it up and dismiss the whole enterprise. Finally, do we drink the water deeply and gratefully, or thoughtlessly; do we use it carelessly, spilling or wasting it, or do we always give it to others and not drink ourselves; do we hoard it or regard it as too precious to be used to quench our thirst?

The Well and its water outlive any one individual or generation; for this reason it is an apt symbol for the Tao, but still the Tao, the Way, lies beyond any symbol or explanation. We can grasp facets of it from the image, but they can only be hints. Ursula Le Guin, in her commentary on Number 55 in the *Tao Te Ching*, writes, 'The Way is more than the cycle of any individual life. We rise, flourish, fail. The Way never fails. We are waves. It is the sea' (Le Guin, 1997). Yet the image of the well embodies an essential truth: it is only through the 'thirst' of the individual human being who seeks wisdom, peace, understanding or the end of suffering that the water of the Tao can be found and tasted. Without that connection, made through greater and greater consciousness or awareness, we remain inwardly and outwardly divided, our integrity compromised, drawing on changeable and transient resources for our security and nourishment. The Well is one of the most important and challenging of the hexagrams in the *I Ching*.

The Changing Lines

6/1st   We enter the hexagram with this line, and it is similar to the well itself. This is where the pure water of the spring is first collected. We would not consider constructing a well where the water is muddy or polluted; it would be better to use the available time to seek for a purer source. This line counsels us to look at things as they are, not as we would have them be. This requires honesty and a willingness to wait in order to forge a strong and lasting first link in the chain.

9/2nd   Sometimes we hope so much for an early sign that we are on the right course that when it doesn't materialize – at least, not in a form that we can recognize – we become disheartened and may even consider turning our back on our quest. So much may be invested in the search for answers that we cannot imagine carrying on after this initial disappointment. In fact, we need to become familiar with this experience, as it will be repeated again and again. If we learn how to yield and become still in the face of obstacles and setbacks, then the way forward will take on a rhythm of its own. The pauses then become an integral part of the whole, offering us fresh opportunities for reflection and choice.

9/3rd   At a certain moment we may become aware of an alignment having happened. Something seems to 'click'; instead of feeling alienated and confused, we begin to find reflections of ourselves around us, a match between our deepest hunger and what is offered. As our own flow joins the deep flow of the Tao, we may experience life with a new intensity, feel a new urgency. In order for the energy of what is happening to become a lasting resource, we need to create space for stillness and thoughtfulness. The water of the well is drawn up by an ordinary wooden bucket; whatever the equivalent of this object and this activity is in our lives, we should not neglect it.

6/4th   Sometimes, without seeking it or quite understanding how it happened, we find ourselves in the position of serving as a 'well' for others. Of course, this is a normal part of the give and take of life, but if it escalates to the point that we are becoming drained and exhausted, then we must address the situation without delay. Our first concern should be for ourselves; we may need to take time off, time for healing and rest and, above all, time to collect ourselves. Others may need to learn how to become resource-full for themselves.

9/5th   No matter how deep and well-built a well is, if the water is not constantly refreshed by springs it will lose its health-giving properties. The comparison with human life and wisdom is obvious: no matter how much we might have achieved, or how high we might have risen, if we are not renewed and nourished by a deep connection to an inexhaustible source we, too, will become 'stagnant' and will have nothing to give to others. The wise person knows this and never goes for long without time for retreat and re-creation.

6/top   The purpose of the well is to serve; when it fulfils that purpose it *is* a well; until then it is just an idea of a well that exists in our minds. Our purpose is also to serve through taking on the form of what we each individually and uniquely have it within us to become.

49. Ko / Revolution (Moulting)

Primary Trigrams

above *Tui* / The Joyous, Lake
below *Li* / The Clinging, Fire

Nuclear Trigrams

above *Ch'ien* / The Creative, Heaven
below *Sun* / The Gentle, Wood, Wind

The hexagram Revolution portrays the powerful forces of change: upper primary trigram *Tui*, signifying the Lake or enclosed water, has *Li*, Fire, below it. In addition, nuclear trigram *Sun*, Wind or Wood, increases the effect of the fire and, finally, *Ch'ien*, strongly ascending towards Heaven, draws the wind and fire upwards. Under these conditions the waters of *Tui* will not only become agitated and then boil, they will, if these effects continue, change form altogether and become steam or vapour.

There are times when change occurs more or less spontaneously: for instance, when an animal moults or grows a new shell or skin or a new pair of antlers. Casting off the old may or may not be a painful process under these circumstances; there may or may not be a period of vulnerability or irritability, but one thing is certain, it is necessary. The old has been outgrown and must be replaced, or it will restrict the growth of the living creature and, ultimately, endanger its life.

Sometimes, it seems that the conflicts that attend growth periodically require of us a profound act of accountability, of making conscious all that we have allowed to settle to the bottom of our psyches. A sense of necessity applies not only to the act of renewal or cleansing itself, but also to the apparent violence of it. It must be so in order to guarantee that we do not go back on the change lightly, that it is, in effect, irreversible. Such a change may be the result of a process of long reflection and deliberation, where a serious attempt had been made to limit the damage done to others and where both the timing and the manner in which it is effected reflects well on the judgement and integrity of the individual or individuals involved. Such a degree of measure may only rarely be possible; none the less, we should be careful not to blind ourselves wilfully to the choices we have.

We must not append judgements to catastrophic or revolutionary events that explain them in terms of 'inevitability' (global or even cosmic retribution or reward), but also we must not consider ourselves to be more powerful than we actually are. It is best neither to avoid nor seek such events, but, if the need is undeniable, we should act on our own behalf, not on behalf of others, recognizing that first and foremost it is in our own hearts and minds that that necessity has made itself felt.

Finally, according to Chinese symbology, *Tui* is the sign of the Magician and the Calendar-maker. The individual who could predict seasonal changes and the outcome of events long before less observant individuals might notice the relevant patterns and influences in the heavens or around themselves on earth was seen as a Mage, a Sage. Such men and women were relied upon to tell others when crops should be planted or rituals performed, and thus they carried within them the first 'calendar'. Magic is nothing more than a profound understanding of how the world works and how man may attune himself to those deep workings, for good or ill.

The Changing Lines

Change is something we all both long for and fear. For that reason, timing is often a matter of impulse and frustration rather than of patient observation, reflection, and self-examination. The Changing Lines address the conflict evoked by the promise or threat of change and indicate how and when it might be wise to wait or to make a move.

9/1st   Relationships between individuals (or between different aspects of ourselves) are both similar to and different from those pertaining to the two elements, fire and water. Both must be handled with great respect and understanding, but with human beings we are dealing with a greater degree of complexity and therefore a much more uncertain outcome. Decisions that might have a profound effect should be considered carefully and not rushed. In most cases there is more than enough time to do this reflective work and thus to avoid impulsive action. There may be other ways to effect change that are more relational.

6/2nd   Sometimes, in an attempt to forestall conflict, we take on 'protective colouration', camouflaging our true position or feelings in order to avoid unpleasantness or even schism. This not only compromises our deepest self, it also simply postpones the 'day of reckoning'. The sooner we face the true picture and deal with it honestly, the sooner the whole process will be free to move on.

9/3rd   When momentum for change is felt to be building and the time for action appears to be imminent, we may find ourselves under considerable pressure to make a move. If possible, we should find time to honestly review our position, seeking to discriminate between what is 'ours' and what might belong to 'others'. Our choices should no more be based on resisting the advice of others than it is on blindly following that advice. Not all demands for change – whether originating from within or without – need to be met.

9/4th   When much has already been achieved, and before further change is embarked upon, we may need to pause, perhaps to take the time to consolidate or integrate earlier gains, perhaps simply to step back and recognize this moment and what it signifies. We may need to effect closure on this particular 'chapter', acknowledging what has been accomplished and what has not. If we choose to avoid this phase of the work it may be on account of unresolved issues that will only be carried on into the future, a sort of 'karmic' inheritance that increases with our refusal to 'see' it.

9/5th   Anarchy is revolution without government. If we choose to allow change to happen (to us or to others) without taking cognizance of its force or direction or motivation, then its outcome may well be dangerous or chaotic and will certainly need conscious and responsible work at some point to stabilize the energies involved. However, if we can manage to restrain the urge towards action while supporting the visionary instinct, we may find that these energies will lead to a new and dynamic time in which much is possible.

6/top   Whatever the nature of the desired change, whether revolutionary or moderate, whether within an individual or within society, if it leads to more openness and transparency, it has accomplished much. As we grow older we become increasingly aware of that which unites us, our common humanity; by comparison, those attitudes or attributes that separate us seem ephemeral.

50. Ting / The Cauldron

Primary Trigrams

above *Li* / The Clinging, Fire
below *Sun* / The Gentle, The Penetrating, Wind, Wood

Nuclear Trigrams

above *Tui* / The Joyous, Lake
below *Ch'ien* / The Creative, Heaven

The challenge implied in the imagery and associations of this hexa-gram is how to embrace both that which we are capable of shaping and changing in the allotted space of our lives and also that which we cannot alter, that will cause us to suffer if we cannot accept it. In embracing both we do not differentiate between them, regarding both as essential to our journey, to the expression of our unique creativity. We each have a lifetime of choices to make, but we need to be continually aware of the spirit in which we make them and of the ways in which our actions and choices reach beyond us in their consequences.

The hexagram pictures the ancient Chinese vessel, the *Ting*. The divided lines in the first and fifth positions are seen as the feet and the carrying handles of the *Ting*, respectively. The primary trigrams of *Sun*, Wood and *Li*, Fire further illustrate the image of a cooking vessel on the fire. In fact, the *Ting* was a ceremonial vessel, not used for ordinary cooking, and consequently, this hexagram symbolizes much more than might be immediately obvious.

The force and nature of elementary Fire (*Li*) defies description. *This* fire is specific to Now, yet the word, 'Fire' so fundamentally defines the created universe that we cannot speak of the former without implying the latter. Further, human culture is virtually synonymous with the use of fire, for cooking, for agriculture, as a focus (the Latin word for hearth) for social interaction, as a threat to large predators, and, perhaps most important of all, simply to light the darkness; consequently, *Ting* also refers to the growth of culture and civilization.

But the hexagram suggests more than that as well: the vessel itself represents life in its broadest sweep, human life, both in general, as in the growth of culture, and also each personal life, and even beyond that, the very force that is Life, continuous and unified, co-existing with the universe, beyond the limits of time or space, unconditioned. When we say 'my' life, we are speaking of the formal or temporal vessel of a particular physical body, but it is we who are possessed by life; we do not possess it. Life is what we are; what we do with that is, partly, the result of the opportunities and limitations that we encounter and partly – perhaps the greater part – the result of differing capacities for endurance, growth, creativity, hope, equanimity, and commitment. In terms of this hexagram, we can shape our life into an ordinary cooking pot and live perfectly happily, or we can make of it a 'Ting', a vessel for the transformation of the ordinary into the transcendental. As with the alchemists, the 'lead' of our lives may be transmuted into 'gold', or, rather, the gold that Life is may be discovered hidden in the apparent 'lead' of its formal, conditioned appearance. All this is contained in the imagery of the *Ting*.

The time pictured in this hexagram is Now, this moment, never before and never again to exist. 'Now' is the only time we ever really have in which to act and choose. 'Now' is the continual challenge in which every situation and every choice is made anew, made as if for the first time. The deeper our connection to Life in all its forms, as well as in its ultimate formlessness, the greater will be our ability to live gratefully and creatively.

The Changing Lines

6/1st   If, as this hexagram suggests, it is a time for renewal or recommitment, the first step must be to consciously empty ourselves of old ideas or attitudes, releasing them in preparation for the new or the unexpected; putting new wine in old bottles has been recognized as a bad idea for a long time. No matter what follows, we have actively signalled our willingness to be 'used'. Although in a sense this is a decision to become more yin – open and yielding, perhaps unselfish – it requires a degree of perceptiveness, clarity, and determination that can only come from the gathered consciousness of a self-aware individual.

9/2nd At times it may seem hardly worthwhile making the effort to live a meaningful life in the face of the sure knowledge of death. The Bible tells us to 'Take no thought for the morrow . . .', yet human beings are rarely good at living without anxiety about death, loss, or illness. This line reminds us that life is like a moving flame; we cannot alter the reality of the brevity of life, but we can learn to be still with it, to make of our lives a thing of beauty and brilliance. We can learn to release more readily, to move on from experiences of pain or joy rather than getting stuck in them or fearing to let them go.

9/3rd This strong line lies in the transitional third position and represents a moment of choice or even crisis. We may be on the brink of an important resolution to an outer or inner situation, yet recognize neither how sensitive conditions are at this juncture nor how much has already been accomplished. Danger and opportunity are the two sides of the 'coin' of crisis. Fatigue or restlessness could lead us to do something impulsive, or, conversely, we might convince ourselves that really it does not matter if we complete the work now or at some other time. Very little may separate us from the fruition of all that has gone before, but if we move carelessly this moment could be lost. Above all, we must steady ourselves and get back in touch with what actually is.

9/4th The individual represented by this line now finds himself in a difficult position and he should stop and reflect. Essentially, the problems or obstacles that now face him are not of his own making, yet the resolution of these problems has been given to him to achieve. He may well feel frustrated by what seems to be a diversion from his path; however, this work will define the continuing path as it does this moment on the path. This is a difficult time and presents a great challenge to the individual.

6/5th All work of a transformative or creative nature requires total commitment and yet is never completed for once and for all. This may feel daunting, but it may also be a relief: we can only do what we are capable of at any given time; it doesn't have to be perfect; there will always be another opportunity and another and another. This line reminds us simply that gain and loss and the cycles of inspiration and emptiness are the essence of the creative process as they are of life. If we can remember this, then when we find ourselves 'right back at the beginning' with a sense of having achieved nothing, we might be better able to let go of all such measures or judgements.

9/top Life is refreshed and rejuvenated by the entry of wild or unexpected elements. Sometimes we equate maturity with seriousness and gravity, yet often those who have achieved a degree of wisdom delight in the new, the strange, the 'wacky'. The richness of untamed energies vitalizes us all. Those who are truly open to, and curious about, all of life – the ordinary as well as the extraordinary – have a lightness of being that makes them seem to be almost transparent.

51. Chên / The Arousing, Thunder

Primary Trigrams

above *Chên* / The Arousing, Thunder
below *Chên* / The Arousing, Thunder

Nuclear Trigrams

above *K'an* / The Abysmal, Water
below *Kên* / Keeping Still, Mountain

Chên is one of the eight hexagrams formed by doubling one of the primary trigrams. *Chên* stands in the East and represents spring and morning and vitality. It stands for the rousing sounds of thunder and music. In the *Shuo Kua* (see Appendix A) we find, 'God comes forth in the sign of the Arousing . . .'. *Chên* is the first offspring of the undifferentiated, primal elements of *Ch'ien*, Heaven and *K'un*, Earth; its arrival is the first 'event' (we could even call it the 'Big Bang'), a cataclysmic and mysterious arising, apparently out of 'thin air'. Such tremendous energy is terrifying and shocking, as we know from the experience of earthquakes, volcanic eruptions, hurricanes. The forces represented by *Chên* have always attracted us; they know no moderation and are untempered by reflection or restraint.

We may well experience events in our lives that have the same effect as these natural cataclysms, events that completely disrupt or even destroy the rhythm and familiarity of our relationships or our sense of who we are or what life is about. At such a time it is more important than ever to observe or establish some sort of small ritual that serves as a witness to the profound nature of the change or challenge taking place. Without this human effort that seeks to find a personally meaningful way of viewing the situation as it unfolds, we can easily become lost and paralysed. Ritual represents a choice for awareness, calm, and connectedness to the wider mystery within which these particular events are evolving; by embracing both the known and the unknown elements, it affords containment, and can settle and centre us. This holds true for extremely exciting and promising moments as well as for more difficult or overwhelming ones.

Chên represents such a powerful initiatory energy or drive that issues of leadership are very naturally associated with it. The requirements of a great leader, explored frequently in the I Ching, are the same now as in the distant Chinese past: integrity, vision, generosity, courage, wisdom. When the need for leadership is very great, there is a corresponding danger of turning to a less excep-tional, even inadequate, individual who offers simplistic solutions to complex problems.

The Changing Lines

9/1st   This is the first expression of the force of The Arousing. It is powerful and shocking, and its energy needs to be 'earthed' through understanding its meaning and also through 'grounding' it in ordinary, day to day life. In other words, great events must first be recognized as significant and then be followed up by choices and actions that channel the energy. Otherwise, that energy may drain away or be dissi-pated through inaction or indecision.

6/2nd Sometimes we need to be told simply to 'grow up'. We cannot afford to become passive in the face of powerful or shocking events, or to be victimized by them. Even if there is little that we can actively do, we still owe it to ourselves to practise self-awareness. Times of loss or change may offer us a rare and important opportunity to take responsi-bility for our own lives, to become more real while at the same time confronting and reflecting on more profound issues than we are generally called upon to consider.

6/3rd Different people react in different ways to powerful, signifi-cant, or shocking events. Some people are not prepared to move into exciting times because they are afraid that the outcome will not be perfect. Others may be fearful that they will lose all they have worked hard to gain. When we become anxious about the future, we lose our capacity for both joy and clear-sighted judgement. We become indecisive and over-cautious. We need to learn to live mindfully but also energetically. There is a line in T. S. Eliot's 'Ash Wednesday' that reads, 'Teach us to care and not to care . . .'.

9/4th   Often, in the midst of a particular situation or set of circumstances, a moment comes that we recognize as critical, possibly even a turning point. At such a time we must give real consideration to our choices within the situation. The times will support us if we choose courageously, but the promise inherent in this moment could be destroyed if we act recklessly. The way forward requires both trust and care.

6/5th   At times it is best to simply and deliberately yield to events, to 'rest' in the situation and be carried by it rather than resisting or reacting to it, or by attempting to seize back control. However, we should not underestimate the effect that such a decision may have on others, and we need to stay actively attuned to small but significant changes in the overall picture.

6/top   When events fail to reach a natural conclusion, we, or others, may be unconsciously blocking such closure. The fact that this is not being done consciously can lead to considerable confusion and agitation and the situation must be addressed. We must seek clarification and not assume that eventually all will be well. It may not be in our power to resolve the difficulties, but we should consider it our responsibility to become as aware as possible of any role that we might be playing inadvertently. Beyond that we should simply stay in place.

52. Kên / Keeping Still, Mountain

Primary Trigrams

above *Kên* / Keeping Still, Mountain
below *Kên* / Keeping Still, Mountain

Nuclear Trigrams

above *Chên* / The Arousing, Thunder
below *K'an* / The Abysmal, Water

Kên is one of the eight hexagrams formed by doubling a primary trigram, in this case *Kên*, Keeping Still, Mountain. When trigrams are doubled, we recognize a two-fold emphasis, the lower trigram representing a more physical or materialistic focus and the upper trigram representing a more thoughtful or spiritual focus. Of course, these are simply two expressions of a single idea, but it can help at times to have the idea illustrated in different modes. Keeping still physically means quietening the body, slowing down, perhaps actually stopping, becoming like a mountain, broad-based, rooted, solid. Keeping still mentally or spiritually means quietening the mind, slowing the endless streams of thought that assail us continuously with fears about the past or the future, imaginings that prevent us from experiencing the stillness at the heart of the present moment.

Quietness of the heart and stillness of the mind have been sought for probably as long as human beings have been conscious. While some individuals have always found this experience of profound peace in nature or wilderness, many others over the centuries have pursued the path of prayer and meditation. No matter what route we may choose, the goal is essentially the same, to be able to rest quietly in the body, in the present moment, without anxiety and without hope. Anxiety causes us to worry about either the consequences of some action in the past or about some feared or desired outcome in the future. Hope undermines our capacity to accept and dwell in the present moment. Hope, as T. S. Eliot puts it, is generally hope 'for the wrong thing' (Eliot, 1963): it concerns a 'better' future moment; it is rarely neutral and cannot co-exist with stillness, which is, at heart, the same as acceptance. The most profound stillness comes when we can let go of hopes, fears, and anxieties and be rooted in what is, right now. Then this moment expands into a boundless and welcoming space of quiet abundance and sufficiency.

Kên stands in the northeast of the compass, and its positioning has led it to be associated with the mysterious place of transformation where endings become beginnings and the greatest achievement of life, wisdom, finally becomes unified with the Tao. The stillness of Kên that is the goal of all seeking – 'the peace that passeth understanding' – then gives way to Chên, The Arousing, that stands in the east. These two hexagrams are intimately connected: the truest action arises out of, but is always rooted in, stillness. Stillness, on the other hand, derives its power from the effective concentration of energy that occurs when mental and physical activity are quietened.

Finally, stillness taken to an extreme leads to paralysis. Balance is always essential and the heaviness of the Mountain may, at times, be more leaden and death-like than peaceful.

The Changing Lines

6/1st   Experience teaches us that true peace comes from inside and is the achievement of a lifetime; however, we have to start somewhere and each step is important, even if in itself it will not provide all the answers. We start when we put the intention into practice and, no matter how small that first step is, it is significant. Ultimately, we learn that outward 'show' of knowledge or achievements does not bring a quiet heart; that comes from letting go of the need to impress others.

6/2nd   At times we need to confront and renegotiate attitudes or ways of coping that we developed at another time for different reasons. From a superficial perspective, passivity or paralysis, stagnation or contraction can appear similar to stillness; the difference is that these are defensive attitudes informed by fear or anger. If a position traps us and limits our responses, then it is counter-productive to our growth. Stillness expands the heart and mind.

9/3rd   Our path forward is always into the unknown. As much as we may try to hold on to certainties and a sense of knowing where we are going, nothing is ever certain. Growth involves releasing the past – even releasing the present – over and over again. It is entirely natural that we become paralysed at times and feel that the choices we make are the determinants of the future. In fact, life has a way of bringing us back to ourselves, to familiar conflicts or questions, and giving us another and another opportunity to experiment and learn. If, on a daily basis, we take time to remind ourselves that we are in a process and the goal is unknown and, in a sense, unknowable, then we may be able to make our choices quietly and fearlessly. Becoming still is often the same as stopping struggling.

6/4th   The most important aspect of stillness is that it should be full of breath and breathing, not contracted. When circumstances change or threaten us with the new or the unknown, it is natural to 'hold' our breath rather than to breathe deeply, relaxing into each intake of breath, releasing into each exhalation. If we can do this, then we take our stillness with us. Remaining quiet and not becoming anxious or doubtful when we find ourselves far from 'home' is not easy, but the less 'baggage' we are carrying the easier it will be.

6/5th   It is not a bad thing to aim high, but if we are in a rush to achieve our goals we may become easily disappointed when things don't go our way. The more difficult or challenging the path we have chosen, the more important it will be to balance measurable growth with the less visible but essential growth of patience and endurance – the 'roots' that keep us firmly grounded and nourished. The temptation to over-reach ourselves needs to be quietly monitored, not fearfully, but out of a sense of responsibility to whatever vision inspires us.

9/top   Agitation of the heart and mind and body is simply part of living and growing and loving life and what it has to offer;

however, as we mature we learn that the greatest gifts come unbidden, that all we have to do is open ourselves as fully as possible to every day and every encounter or experience. The pressing need for recognition, achievement, or excitement that may have dominated our lives before disappears. In its place gratitude, delight, appreciation, and acceptance can begin to flower.

53. Chien / Development (Gradual Progress)

Primary Trigrams

above *Sun* / The Gentle, Wood, Wind
below *Kên* / Keeping Still, Mountain

Nuclear Trigrams

above *Li* / The Clinging, Fire
below *K'an* / The Abysmal, Water

This hexagram pictures a tree growing on the top of a mountain. The tree is exposed in such a position and, if it is to survive, it will need to adapt to the extreme conditions that prevail. First and foremost, it must establish deep and strong roots. The growth of such a tree may be stunted in comparison with what might be possible in a more benign position, but it could outlive the tree that grows without hardship. Trees that grow in isolated places often become landmarks, their characteristic shape or outline on a hill being recognizable from afar and serving as a point of orientation in the landscape.

It is not difficult to relate this image to human life. There are times when growth is bound to be slow because we are more exposed and vulnerable than usual. At such times wisdom lies in looking to our rootedness; it is not a time for reckless acts in defiance of the prevailing conditions. Growth takes place out of sight and we become the stronger for it. Such times require considerable courage, as others may not recognize or understand the reasons behind the choices we need to make as we adapt and put down roots into the dark earth. We need nourishment – material and spiritual – adequate for this task of enduring, and it may be a time when we find new sources of enlightenment, support, or guidance. Emerging from such a time we may discover that it has been highly significant to our development even though it has felt as if we have done nothing but submit.

The hexagram has also been associated with enduring relationships. They, too, develop slowly, tested by events and experiences over the years, each developing its own characteristic 'shape'. There can be no ideal shape when we are considering individuals or their relationships: beauty lies not in conventional forms but in the more subtle and unique transparency that we may take on if we allow ourselves to respond to the deepest movements of Life within and without.

The Changing Lines

6/1st In the same way that the roots of a mountain lie deep within the earth, so our roots in the past – both personal and collective – shape our growth and all our multiple beginnings. Early experiences of give-and-take may play a role in shaping our willingness to adapt. If we have experienced patience and support through early difficulties, we will be more able to draw on those experiences and attend to the requirements of the present. If not, we may find it difficult to believe in ourselves or our personal vision. A degree of insight into our foundation experiences can be a great help.

6/2nd Matching our response to the demands of the moment and then releasing that moment safeguards both our energy and our spontaneity. It enables us to rest between the challenges of life and also to persevere on our path. It also means we are living fully in the present, unencumbered by worries about the past or the future. These are the best possible conditions for the flowering of individual potential.

9/3rd A moment comes in our development, if we are seeking real growth, when we find ourselves having to 'stick [our] head above the parapet'; in other words, become visible, with all the potential for adulation or attack which that implies. Another familiar image for the challenge of such a time is, 'sticking one's neck out', making oneself vulnerable, risking exposure, 'pinning one's colours to the mast'. We need to trust that we have done the vital work and that we stand to gain from risking exposure in this way.

6/4th   After every new achievement we need to allow time for the new growth to mature before we expose it to difficult conditions. If we rush this period of stabilization we subject the new thing to trials for which it may not be sufficiently robust. Sometimes this is unavoidable, but at least we can recognize the situation and seek to stay well grounded until this particular time passes, not over-extending ourselves unnecessarily.

9/5th   In the terms of the hexagram, we need to recognize when we have achieved as much as we need to achieve in the 'outer' world, when the time has come to turn inwards instead. This may prove to be a harder path than that which we have trodden previously, requiring patience and a capacity to stay with uncertainty and not try to resolve or 'fix' it.

9/top   Throughout life, fears about ageing and death may preoccupy or even overwhelm us. This should not be seen as morbid or unhealthy, but rather as a natural preparation for that which we all face at the end of our lives. Our bodies are changing all the time and our sense of *who* we are is intertwined with our apprehensions about *how* we are and *how* we appear to others. These thoughts and experiences can challenge us deeply and become real obstacles to growth. As we mature we experience again and again the truth that the only growth that is worth having is that which is achieved through going deeply into Life, surrendering to it and rooting oneself in its energy.

54. Kuei Mei / The Marrying Maiden

Primary Trigrams

above *Chên* / The Arousing, Thunder
below *Tui* / The Joyous, Lake

Nuclear Trigrams

above *K'an* / The Abysmal, Water
below *Li* / The Clinging, Fire

'The Marrying Maiden' takes its name from the imagery of *Tui*, the youngest daughter, following *Chên*, the oldest son, who may be giving his sister in marriage to another man or who may, himself, be the bridegroom. The suggestion is that this young woman will now take her place in society and leave childhood behind. In a more generalized interpretation we can explore this hexagram as a representation of the course of life and of personal development, addressing issues of order and disorder or the formal and the spontaneous. *Tui* symbolizes joy and youth, and she follows *Chên*, who, as the oldest son, is responsible for ritual and for the observance of tradition and custom, a very conservative figure. The young are often characterized as headstrong, impatient with forms and their restraints, eager to experience pleasure, to fashion their own meanings, create their own order. Naturally enough, this unrestrained energy can easily be perceived as a threat. But life embraces opposing energies without difficulty, and this hexagram explores all aspects of the imagery of youth and age and, more particularly, of maturity and immaturity.

The four trigrams which constitute *Kuei Mei* represent the four cardinal points and the four seasons: North and winter, *K'an*; South and summer, *Li*; East and spring, *Chên*; West and autumn, *Tui*. In addition, *K'an* symbolizes the moon and *Li* the sun. The hexagram mirrors the cosmos and emphasizes the importance of becoming aware of our inner points of orientation, of how we naturally 'position' ourselves, where we feel most comfortable or uncomfortable, and why. Participating fully in life requires that we grow up and develop our understanding of the part we play in determining our path, rather than seeing ourselves as powerless and incapable of shaping our own destiny.

The hexagram reminds us of the tension between individual choice and collective responsibility and mores. We do not have to sacrifice curiosity and the spirit of adventure to the staid pursuit of constancy, but nor should we blind ourselves to the wholeness and interdependency of life. This is the balance – and these are the choices – with which *Kuei Mei* confronts us.

The Changing Lines

9/1st   There are few questions that we return to again and again throughout life; perhaps the most common one concerns our place in the cosmos. From the time they can speak, children express curiosity about where and how we fit in. If we avoid this area it is out of fear, fear about ageing, insignificance, and death. One sign of maturity is if we are able to address and overcome our fears and engage with this most fascinating and challenging question.

9/2nd   It is not easy to bear feelings of insignificance and we do not make it easier for ourselves if we attempt to hang on to control and a sense of power in order to avoid discomfort. The balance between recognition of our relative powerlessness – represented by the fact of personal death – and our freedom to choose and to create our lives is one that we must continually negotiate. Every day presents us with opportunities to review to what extent we are forcing events or, on the other hand, being moved by them. The interaction between yin and yang is always shifting, both within and without.

6/3rd   If we can acknowledge and accept that our individual strength will always be lesser than, and contingent upon, the greater strengths and rhythms of nature, we may become more able to 'seize the day' fearlessly. Sometimes we hesitate out of fear of where our ambitions will lead us, but the alternative to trusting such energies is to miss out on life. Of course, we risk attracting competition as well as not achieving all we envisioned, but we learn through experience rather than through imaginings.

9/4th   We all wonder at times if we will ever learn or ever manage to attain wisdom, or ever be able to realize our dreams, or ever get 'anywhere'. Indeed, we may wonder if we have achieved anything at all. So much growth goes on out of sight, growth that we cannot measure or evaluate, but that bears fruit if we can just persevere on our path. Comparing ourselves to others never works; what we each have to bring forth out of the particular conditions of our own lives will always be unique. However, this is not a counsel for isolated individuality; the support, encouragement, advice, and example of others is vital throughout life.

6/5th   Taking the result as the path is a liberating Buddhist teaching. Perseverance and equanimity are combined, linking the happy acceptance of whatever outcome arises with the capacity for patient effort. This allows us to release experiences easily, even if they have seemed negative. Equanimity is an achievement that requires – and results in – openness, thoughtfulness, and generosity. It is not that nothing touches us, but rather that everything does, and we learn gradually how to embrace it and not be overwhelmed by it.

6/top   The conditions of life are such that we will always be challenged to handle situations that are difficult for us. Life does not proceed in a straight line but rather in a spiral. We revisit old experiences and old problematic areas and slowly learn different and more developed ways of dealing with them. With any luck, we will learn to recognize and discern our patterns of response or reaction and will become both more patient with ourselves and also more able to handle the inevitable conflicts of life.

55. Fêng / Abundance

Primary Trigrams

above *Chên* / The Arousing, Thunder
below *Li* / The Clinging, Fire

Nuclear Trigrams

above *Tui* / The Joyous, Lake
below *Sun* / The Gentle, The Penetrating, Wind, Wood

There are two ways of considering 'Abundance': the first is as an external set of favourable conditions and the second is as an internal capacity or predisposition. The first is the more traditional understanding, and is reflected in the attributes of brightness, even brilliance, and energetic motion associated with *Li* and *Chên*. As is often the case, this imagery refers to the promise of rain heralded by thunder (*Chên*) and lightning (*Li*). The promised abundance lies in the future – good crops and the possibility of health and sufficiency for the family or community. But it is incumbent on the farmers and workers to make the most of the rains when they do come and to gather, store, and make wise use of the resulting harvest. The principle of responsibility and participation in the process is taken for granted. There is an association of brevity or transience with this hexagram and the times it portrays. The familiar saying, 'Make hay while the sun shines', often interpreted purely opportunistically and superficially, points to the truth that we should act with vigour when conditions smile on us and both enjoy the present and look to the future, not anxiously but with foresight.

The second way of approaching this hexagram is through its nuclear trigrams, *Sun* and *Tui*. As wind, *Sun* is able to move easily, to adapt itself to obstacles and to touch every part of the world. As wood, *Sun* can put down its yielding 'roots' (lowest line of the trigram) and grow almost anywhere, slowly and with perseverance.

Tui represents the cheerful person whose readiness to experience joy can sustain and support her through difficult times. If we have developed the qualities of adaptability, perseverance, and equanimity, abundance as a state of mind and heart is freed from dependence on favourable external conditions. It lies instead in a capacity to enter life fully, whatever the situation, whatever physical or emotional challenges it presents. The relative desirability of one sort of experience over another is a minor concern; disappointment rarely occurs, because no investment has been made in a particular experience or outcome. Life is allowed to be; there is no resistance to any part of it, and so it proceeds in an interesting and connected way: one thing leads to another. True abundance is recognized rather than gained, and it is easily lost if we treat it as a personal possession and try to hold on to it. Unshared abundance is not only distasteful, it is life-denying.

Finally, the opposite of abundance is depletion. It may be that the absence of abundance, of a sense of plenty or of the basic goodness of life, needs to be the focus of our reflection at this time.

The Changing Lines

9/1st   If the early signs are good it does not mean we should throw caution and thrift aside; however, neither should we wilfully reject the promise of possible abundance. We can be strangely reluctant to acknowledge and accept bounty; often we retreat from it as if it were a dangerous offering – a Trojan horse. This faintheartedness does not serve us well and it is likely to continue to sabotage our capacity for gracious acceptance and enjoyment of what is on offer. We risk becoming closed and fragile in our interactions with the world.

6/2nd The combination of openness and determination is an effective one at a time of abundance; it indicates that we are serious, patient, and relatively transparent in terms of our motivation or agenda. There is a small chance that we may be too absorbed in what we see as our task to recognize that we are being carried by an energy that is outside our personal control. It is as if we need to raise our head rather more frequently and notice the goodness or beauty that already exists.

9/3rd   In the same way as we might be aware of the moment when the sun passes its zenith and first begins to turn towards darkness, we might also sense the moment when expansion has almost reached its limit; we recognize that soon it will shift and reverse its direction. While some may prefer to gradually close down whatever project they were engaged in at this point, others may choose to open themselves to the energies of the moment, possibly releasing their earlier agenda and trusting that, come what may, they stand to gain from the experience.

9/4th   As we move through life we revise our definition of abundance; gradually, the balance shifts towards a less material emphasis than when we were young. When one definition begins to become outdated, we may pass through a difficult time when we do not know what we are hoping for or what it would look like if it came to us. This can happen at any age. At such a time we can benefit from a period of rest, of relative invisibility and few demands. We are vulnerable, and need time in which to come apart in safety before coming together again.

6/5th   Sometimes, individuals or groups that have worked in harmony for a period of time suddenly begin to manifest conflict, and this can lead to open hostility or even schism. If this occurs within an individual, he may experience tremendous stress as he struggles to maintain coherence. It is not surprising that this happens, as growth necessarily involves us in defining ourselves in terms of what we are not. At a later stage we may resume harmonious relations, but for the present we need to respect the process of self-development and differentiation. Such conflicts cannot be resolved in any conventional way, because they arise out of the continuous interplay of the opposites.

6/top   A sense of abundance that relies on outer conditions will inevitably wax and wane. As with all temporal phenomena it is transient, continually shifting and changing. The loss of a sense of plenty may throw us back on ourselves and challenge us to seek a new alignment within. It may also illuminate something we overlooked because it drew no attention to itself – a different sort of brilliance.

56. Lü / The Wanderer (The Outsider)

Primary Trigrams

above Li / The Clinging, Fire
below Kên / Keeping Still, Mountain

Nuclear Trigrams

above Tui / The Joyous, Lake
below Sun / The Gentle, Wood, Wind

This hexagram pictures fire on a mountain. Burning vigorously, it does not linger long in one place but moves on quickly. It is highly visible in the same way as a stranger – a 'wanderer' – is visible. The wanderer is a solitary person who is disinclined to put down roots and get established in a community or in a role. Freedom of movement and expression means he does not become identified with a particular place or opinion. At the same time, he may be regarded with some suspicion: as an outsider he cannot be relied upon to behave in a predictable manner. Those who have chosen a more collective and traditional lifestyle may be uneasy with his independence.

This figure is enigmatic, not easily grasped or known, and he is unsettling for us in that he resists the temptation to become comfortable and to 'belong', a fundamental need that practically defines human society. However, probably all of us experience some urge to 'wander' at some time in our lives, to be a stranger, anonymous. We long to be free to move on, to start again, but we do not want to offend anybody. We feel grateful for the warmth and support offered to us by our friends and family, but do not want it to tie us down. The Wanderer inside each of us is the Other who does not respond to the same calls as we do, or as we have learnt to do. He/she does not seek closeness, approval, or admiration, has no need of the familiar, no desire to accumulate possessions. The

Other stands for another way, a more difficult and lonely way that involves a journey away from 'home' and the learning of a new type of conduct.

We can learn something from the attitude of the Wanderer; we can learn to value our time here and not take it for granted. After all, we are not here for long in this lifetime, then we move on. The nuclear trigrams *Sun* and *Tui* point to the importance of the qualities of gentleness and joyousness, and the primary trigrams indicate that even in the midst of movement we must be still, like the mountain, not restlessly moving on but releasing ourselves to life. *Li*, the flame, emphasizes the message: let your light burn with brilliance, but also be clear-sighted and recognize that life is brief.

While the central idea of the hexagram may be to 'lighten up', to move on, to release whatever is weighing us down, to explore, learn new ways, get new views, there is another way of looking at it, and that is from the point of view of somebody who has been a wanderer all his life and for whom the greatest challenge is that of stopping, putting down roots, and recognizing that life must be lived here and now. Perhaps, in summary, we could see this hexagram as indicating that it is time to 'visit' the areas of ourselves and life that have remained unknown to us; time to shake free from anything that deadens life.

The Changing Lines

6/1st   If the main thrust of the time requires us to move beyond the known and the easy, then a hesitant start may not be sufficiently determined to overcome resistance or fear, particularly if we are naturally reticent about change and the unknown. There is a wonderful story from *Desert Wisdom* in which a careful and conscientious novice monk comes to Abba Joseph and asks what more he can do. He is already fasting and praying and observing every detail of the practice. 'The old man stood up and stretched out his hands towards heaven, and his fingers became like ten torches of flame. And he said, "If you wish, you can become all flame"' (Nomura, 1983).

6/2nd   As long as we do not resist life it will take us on paths we could not have foreseen; all we need to do is say, 'Yes' to what arises. If we consciously dedicate our choices, actions, and intentions to the furtherance of the general good or the lessening of suffering, this can help in overcoming personal inhibitions. It is all too easy for us to feel that our choices are insignificant in the overall scheme of life, and this practice honours a deeper reality and affirms the centrality of every human being.

9/3rd   It is never too late to try something different, explore new territory, expand our horizons. The difficulty may lie in a fear of being visible, making an obvious 'mistake' and having others see it. Fears such as these, based in the experience of shame, can paralyse us for a lifetime and must be taken on by choosing to act fearlessly, even if we do not feel fearless.

9/4th   There could be any number of reasons to make the choice for stopping, some courageous, some realistic, some anxious, some from a deep sense of the 'rightness' of that choice. There is a 'Wanderer' in each of us, but the extent to which we live that potential will vary. The choices we make shift us between contraction and expansion, between being apart from the general flow and being part of that flow; these movements constitute the rhythm of life.

6/5th   If we are steadfast in seeking to increase our awareness and our capacity for creative choice, a moment is likely to arrive when we pass a point of no return. Without even realizing it, without seeking it, we find we are in a different relation to everything. If we knew this was coming, would we have travelled so far? The journey beyond this point will be different from what has gone before.

9/top   Sometimes we move just for the sake of keeping going, a dangerous and unrealistic way of proceeding. As soon as we become aware of this we can stop, gather ourselves, and seek to bring to light whatever fear is driving us. Occasionally, fear is useful in making us move away quickly from a dangerous situation, but in general it is a poor basis on which to make decisions as it undermines our capacity for discernment.

57. Sun / The Gentle (The Penetrating, Wind)

Primary Trigrams

above *Sun* / The Gentle, Wind, Wood
below *Sun* / The Gentle, Wind, Wood

Nuclear Trigrams

above *Li* / The Clinging, Fire
below *Tui* / The Joyous, Lake

Sun is one of the eight foundation trigrams, or forces, in the *I Ching*, and represents the way of the Gentle, the way of wind and wood. Inoffensive, acting almost invisibly, able to slip into the narrowest spaces between the tiniest cracks, combining patience and - perseverance to create strength of a different order to that of the mountains or the seas, time is the tool of *Sun*. The lower primary trigram is associated with a more physical or material expression of these qualities, and the upper with a less tangible, perhaps more intuitive or spiritual expression. Notwithstanding its association with gentleness, *Sun* reflects complex – even paradoxical – energies.

Wind and Wood share some characteristics and have others that are particular to each of them, but they come together in the image of the tree whose roots reach down into the earth, spreading and gathering nutrients while their branches reach up into the sky, connecting the wood of earth (*K'un*) with the wind of heaven (*Ch'ien*). This imagery identifies *Sun* as a powerful linking principle or force, free to move within and between different elements. Wood acts on wind to deflect it; wind acts on wood to weed out weak growth, thus contributing to the health of what remains. The words of the Sufi poet Rumi capture the power and beauty of the wind: 'The same wind which uproots trees makes the grasses shine' (Barks & Moyne, 1995)

The line that defines *Sun* is the yielding line in the first position, and this leads to an association with a quality that is difficult to describe in positive terms; it is a willingness not to stand out, not to draw attention to itself. This seems so out of character with the strength we have just been exploring that it deserves mention. In its lowly position, the defining yin line is as close to the earth as it can be. In that position it is utterly rooted and ready for anything. If we consider this in terms of human behaviour, the parallel would be with somebody who does not stand on ceremony, or need to defend her position, or make a particular impression. Such a person is free to move in any direction as she has not constructed her identity from high-profile, highly visible positions, roles, or opinions. She has no investment in the public face of continuity and can, therefore, be true to herself.

In the *Shuo Kua / Discussion of the Trigrams, Sun* is identified as the sign in which all things are 'brought to completion' (see Appendix A); in other words, form itself arises in this sign. The importance of 'fleshing out' words, ideas, or ideals cannot be overemphasized: if we do not embody and make visible that which has come alive within us, we fail ourselves and the whole energy of creation.

Finally, many of us waste a lot of energy wishing the circumstances of our lives were different to what they are. We might as well put chains or weights on ourselves. A tree cannot roam the earth like the wind and the wind cannot sink its roots and grow tall and provide shelter for others as the tree does. To be undistracted by what we cannot be is true freedom.

The Changing Lines

6/1st   At first the picture is of aligned energies working together in a sustained and quietly determined way. In such a case, we might imagine that the ends and the means are equally harmonious. However, whether through impatience or a different view of the process, sometimes we find a division opening up between those who would move faster and those who would move at a more measured pace. Then the alignment slips, whether the division is within ourselves or between us and others. It is not a good idea to force the issue; we need to understand the new dynamic first.

9/2nd If we find ourselves chafing against conditions that seem to be frustrating or restricting our growth or movement towards a goal, it may be that we are working at odds with ourselves on a deeper level. We may need to learn how to adapt, how to bend without feeling we have 'sold out' or been broken. Freedom does not mean unfettered liberty; it means accepting what is and starting where we are.

9/3rd While small earthquakes can release locked-up energies with relative safety, large ones may unleash massively destructive forces. The same is true for us: too much hesitation or self-control can lead to locked-in states of feeling that, if they are released impulsively, may cause harm and have unforeseen consequences. For this reason it is helpful if we can allow ourselves to be continually open to and penetrated by life in all its forms. If we are moved by life we are less likely to become frozen.

6/4th Often we underestimate the influence of the most adaptable and, therefore, most hidden individual or element when things seem to be operating fairly effortlessly. If it/he/she becomes or is replaced by a more rigid, invested, or dynamic element or person, the whole pattern of interaction will be affected and any conflict or confrontation that has been avoided hitherto may now enter the situation from a different quarter with considerable potential for overturning the established order.

9/5th For whatever reason, there are times when we find ourselves up against some sort of block. We may first locate it in the outer world, but, more often than not, the origin of the difficulty lies within. Even if we have achieved a great deal in terms of personal growth and awareness, we are likely to experience periods of stagnation or greater distress. There is work to be done at such a time. Waiting for the block to clear of itself will not do. The effort we invest in discovering and clarifying our deepest fears or desires – particularly, perhaps, around the issue of power – will be repaid by a sense of being at peace with ourselves, reconciled to the past and quieter about the future.

9/top New situations test our adaptability. We all carry old solutions with us; if they work under different circumstances, we might choose to look no further; if not, we will have to seek new solutions. The less fearful we are as we enter unknown territory, the more flexibility we will have. Also, if we can bear in mind that we are only a small part of a much greater whole, it may release us to be 'used' by the new situation in a way that we might not have foreseen but which may result in benefit for others.

58. Tui / The Joyous, Lake

Primary Trigrams

above *Tui* / The Joyous, Lake
below *Tui* / The Joyous, Lake

Nuclear Trigrams

above *Sun* / The Gentle, Wind, Wood
below *Li* / The Clinging, Fire

This is a complex image, and the attributes of *Tui* embrace the opposites perhaps more explicitly than any other of the eight foundation trigrams. First, there is the lake, a boundaried area of water, not like the ocean or the collective unconscious, more like the personal unconscious. The Lake has three types of 'movement', evaporation into the air, where it forms clouds, seepage into the ground, where it joins the ground water (*K'an*) and flooding, when it is unable to accommodate an excess of water. (See Hexagrams 43, *Kuai* / Breakthrough, and 28, *Ta Kuo* / Preponderance of the Great.) It also has the property of reflecting the sky and whatever landscape is around it, including human beings; it is a sort of mirror. The mirroring surface is also a world on which various insects live, and one that bears boats and people. In its depths, beneath its mirror surface, other creatures live in the fallen and rotting debris. Life and death in a lake hinges on the balance between the life-giving nutrients that are stored and carried in the waters and the death-giving grip of too much life that can consume the oxygen, producing stagnation. The continual refreshing of the lake is essential for its health, either through rain or by fresh water pouring in from streams and rivers.

The lake is a microcosm, a framed picture of the world, not the world but a reflection of it. It gives joy because of its capacity to reflect beauty around it and to provide a home for birds and fish and other lake-loving animals. We are refreshed by the sight of a lake. In the hexagram there is an 'inner' lake (the lower primary trigram) and an outer lake (the upper primary trigram), so the idea that the one refreshes the other is explicit in the image, carrying with it the principle that inner joy is of great value to society in general. One joyous person can affect many others in her day to day life and contacts. In particular, *Tui*, as the youngest daughter, brings joy to the whole 'family' as its youngest member, 'the baby'.

Tui represents the mouth and teaching as well as learning through discussion and communication with others, examples of how the inner source of joy and knowledge can benefit the world, but it is also associated with sharp destructiveness. Words used thoughtlessly or cruelly can be extraordinarily wounding. *Tui* also represents the Magician, not surprising considering the capacity of water to create distortions, reflections, and illusions. *Tui*'s action is to make others rejoice, but also to be cutting and destructive – dangerous attributes. *Tui* seems to be the most personal and social of the trigrams.

Finally, joy is a gift, a capacity. At its best, it is transformative, embodied in the individual who seems easy and at one with herself and with the present moment, genuinely friendly towards and quietly curious about whatever happens next, light and responsive, available. At its more fleeting, joy can be contagious, lifting and lightening the moment, possibly helping to transcend real difficulties, breaking, like a ray of sunlight, through dark clouds. As greatly as we need it, joy cannot be sustained indefinitely through effort alone; like the lake that becomes stagnant without fresh water and oxygen, it becomes false and manic, heavy with unacknowledged sadness. True joy sees all and accepts all and lets go.

The Changing Lines

9/1st This strong line in the first position represents self-contained joy that is deep and relatively unaffected by passing phenomena. However, even such a firmly grounded attitude will be tested regularly, otherwise it would have an unreal, manic quality that would inevitably lead to exhaustion. The capacity to embrace both the real trials and sorrows of life and, at the same time, to be surprised by, and rejoice in, life's continuing beauty is a great gift. In spite of everything, with the break of dawn to have one's heart leap, yet again: this is the wonderful quality of profound joy that offers a new start at each moment.

9/2nd The ordinary 'stuff' of life offers us moments in which to rejoice on a daily basis, if we are present enough to perceive them. Ordinary encounters with friends or strangers, animals or aspects of nature, glimpses of beauty or even of sadness – small things. Those who are available in this way seem to be open to the possibilities of each moment, not actively seeking to be 'happy', but with an embodied understanding that 'between the lines' of life there is a steady flow of joy that can be joined at any moment.

6/3rd At times – and unconsciously – we may become invested in sustaining a false optimism or appearance of happiness which then becomes increasingly fragile. This balance cannot hold for long, as the weight of denied reality will eventually render it impossible. When we finally do face the unwanted reality, we may find it is less dire than our inner dread had imagined. In any case, we are then in a position to deal with the situation, as we know from experience that ignoring it is no longer a solution.

9/4th The nature of the pleasures we seek or the joy that finds us shifts over time and throughout life. If we find ourselves no longer particularly enjoying events or experiences that might have satisfied us at one time, it may be a signal to us to consider whether we are looking in the wrong place for happiness, seeking, for instance, quantity rather than quality. Sometimes, if we simplify or 'de-clutter' our lives, we are rewarded with an unexpected quiet joy that we might never have anticipated.

9/5th Many words are used to express happiness: joy, pleasure, cheerfulness, equanimity, gaiety, contentment, and there are more. Some experiences of happiness have a light and naïve quality to them and are fleeting and beautiful; some experiences lead to a profound sense of peace or awe and are described as joyful; some are brittle, manic, and intense. The fifth position in the hexagram is considered to belong to the 'ruler' or 'prince', what we might think of as the individual who has come into some degree of maturity in life. What experiences of joy would we hope for in such a period of our life?

6/top   The wonderful lines from Corinthians are often quoted in the context of maturity or ageing: 'When I was a child, I spake as a child, I thought as a child, I understood as a child; but when I became a man, I put away childish things'. We can continue seeking 'childish' joys right till the end of life, and we may derive much pleasure from that, but there are other satisfactions that might then elude us. One of these arises through the cheerful sharing of all we have with those who will follow us and perhaps replace or outlive us. Through generosity we can sow seeds, at any time of life. This is the highest wisdom.

59. Huan / Dispersion

Primary Trigrams

above *Sun* / The Gentle, The Penetrating, Wind, Wood
below *K'an* / The Abysmal, Water

Nuclear Trigrams

above *Kên* / Keeping Still, Mountain
below *Chên* / The Arousing, Thunder

Huan / Dispersion pictures a warm wind blowing over frozen water – ice – causing it to thaw and break up. It suggests the possibility of deep blockages or 'frozen' states being liberated as they are touched and freed by a new understanding. Looked at from a slightly different perspective, something that should be flowing has become rigid and needs to be approached with gentle curiosity rather than sharp-edged determination or suspicion. Such an open and accepting attitude disperses the 'ice' of fear or anger. Life is continually moving, flowing into different forms that require different responses from us. If we are tight and contracted we cannot move with Life, experiencing its many faces and expanding our own horizons and abilities; instead we are rolled up around ourselves like a frightened creature, unable to see or hear or participate in life.

Sun represents wood as well as wind and, combined with flowing water as represented by *K'an*, a new image emerges, of a wooden boat on the water. The building of a boat used to require many hours of communal labour with a high degree of communication and co-operation. Where misunderstandings or anger have driven individuals into a state of impasse or estrangement, the identification of a common goal towards which everybody can work may represent a way forward, uniting all parties in an endeavour that transcends apparent differences.

Whether motivated by an adventuring spirit, the need to establish new grounds for hunting and agriculture, or on account of
persecution, our human history is one of repeated dispersions. New
centres are formed that continue to articulate and embody the
forms and laws that govern each grouping. Radical change is,
however, unusual, as the essence of being human drives us to form
relationships and seek significance wherever and however we live.
As the seasonal ice is thawed and then reabsorbed into the land or
seas only to reform the following winter, so the dispersion of frozen
or unwanted energies is only part of the process of embracing more
of life. At some point a 'return' must occur in order to complete the
circle and leave nothing outside it.

The Changing Lines

6/1st   The first step in addressing a blockage is to recognize it and
         name it. This can be difficult if the frozen state has become
         generalized and out of reach. A good question to ask
         oneself might be, 'What is my own deepest truth, and am I
         serving and nurturing it at the moment?' Without judging
         or trying to 'fix' it, but with continuing gentleness and
         honesty, it may then become possible to see what it is that
         has stopped flowing. A deeper understanding can then
         evolve. Don't stop until you have got somewhere.
9/2nd   For understanding and reconnection to the essential flow of
         life, rarely do we need to look further than to the ground
         beneath our feet. This is where we are, and if we can accept
         it fully, it will support us and enable a new perspective to
         emerge.
6/3rd   The third position represents the interface between the
         frozen situation and that which is able to thaw it. Working
         through gentleness is the only way; to force something at
         this point will only serve to divide all those concerned,
         whereas this approach will, in time, result in a wholly new
         freedom and outlook.
6/4th   At times, the only way to dissolve a blockage is to accept
         that it cannot be resolved in a way that satisfies everybody.
         This acceptance often opens doors that would not have
         been available otherwise. We must learn over and over

again how to release our attachment to the 'ideal' outcome that we envision and to surrender to what actually is. Only then can a transformation of the 'problem' arise.

9/5th   An entirely new configuration could be the outcome if change is not only allowed but even embraced. This is not a counsel for recklessness, but rather a radical trust in life's creative capacity. This choice – to align oneself with unknown but creative energies – must not be made from a position of weakness or selfishness; if it is, the outcome will reflect the motivation.

9/top   Through a profound alignment with the original 'frozen' condition, a complete, conscious acceptance and identification with it, the whole situation is transformed and liberated. This may prove to be a great challenge.

60. Chieh / Limitation

Primary Trigrams

above *K'an* / The Abysmal, Water
below *Tui* / The Joyous, Lake

Nuclear Trigrams

above *Kên* / Keeping Still, Mountain
below *Chên* / The Arousing, Thunder

K'an represents water in its boundless flowing state, while *Tui* stands for water in its gathered and limited form, the Lake. The nature of *K'an* – its inherent tendency – is to sink, to become groundwater; thus, it will fill the Lake and possibly even flood it. The image points to the importance of a limited receptacle for the boundless, and, as the emphasis in this hexagram is on the vessel rather than on the boundless contents, the discussion of the hexagram explores the nature and importance of limitation. The nuclear trigrams also reflect this focus: while the limitless and ever-renewing energy of *Chên*, the Arousing, surges upwards, *Kên*, the sign of Keeping Still, remains quietly in place, as does the Mountain that *Kên* symbolizes, and serves to limit *Chên*'s primal energy.

The Chinese have always needed to find ways to manage their vast country and its widely dispersed population. In a very real sense the boundless nature of the waters of the earth (*K'an*) is an appropriate metaphor for the Chinese peoples. And *Tui*, with its open line above two firm closed lines, representing the mouth and teaching and, therefore, culture and the organization of society, is an equally appropriate symbol of the necessity for regulation and laws. All activities – social, agricultural or ritual – were highly regulated; there was 'a time for everything' and culture flourished.

By contrast, we have moved away from a high degree of central regulation and have chosen a path where limitation is considered to be a 'bad' thing, a restraint on the realization of human potential and progress. The consequences of this choice are continually debated but are certainly not entirely beneficial. It seems almost irrefutable, if paradoxical, that human beings thrive on a degree of limitation. We can only take so much of the boundless, then, as a lake would were it over-filled, we become flooded. Stress results from lack of containment, lack of boundaries – to the working day, to financial expenditure, to individual expression and achievement. We are encouraged to always seek for 'more', never to be content with what we have already achieved or what is available 'for free'.

The limitless – Life – is only meaningful in its limited embodiment in this individual at this time. If we truly understood this perhaps we would be less careless in our actions and less self-indulgent in our choices.

The Changing Lines

9/1st   Sometimes we react to early constraints with a dangerous heedlessness – a sort of bravado – because we do not want to have to accept the limitations that are imposed right from the start. Here, the new conditions are just beginning to unfold and are largely unknown. The attitude represented by this line is too unfocused, emotional, and unrestrained for the times and might make it more difficult to manage the situation at a later date.

9/2nd Often we can achieve a relatively easy balance between action and restraint that suits our nature and circumstances, but that may not be stable enough to withstand any real challenge. If there is pressure from a more substantial limitation or obstacle, it may provide a real test of conviction and focus.

6/3rd   Challenging times require patience and honesty as well as a degree of imagination. The more of ourselves that we have available at such times, when we must accept waiting and limitation, the more cheerfully will we be able to endure the uncomfortable uncertainty of the present and not resort to impulsive or wish-fulfilling behaviour.

6/4th   Having achieved a balanced attitude consonant with the times, it might seem that the ideal way forward is to acquiesce in limitation and content oneself with living a simple life. There is nothing intrinsically wrong about this attitude, but it could lead to an almost 'unlived' life if potential challenges are consistently avoided. Limitation works when it actually limits something and forces us to focus our minds on what is most important.

9/5th   To align oneself with the times may mean both to work with limitation in order to achieve one's goals and also to release those goals at every moment and allow new energies the space they need to evolve, to shape their own ends. Limitation is no longer an obstacle; it is a choice that enables the greatest possible influx of life's creative potential.

6/top   After a period of limitation, as the requirements of the times begin to change, we are free to return to our usual balance between indulgence and restraint. However, if the times have taught us anything of lasting value, we may hope to emerge as more open, thoughtful, and generous individuals with a greater capacity for self-limitation, equanimity, and compassion. Hardship will then have proved its worth.

61. Chung Fu / Inner Truth

Primary Trigrams

above *Sun* / The Penetrating, Wind, Wood
below *Tui* / The Joyous, Lake

Nuclear Trigrams

above *Kên* / Keeping Still, Mountain
below *Chên* / The Arousing, Thunder

We use the word 'truth' casually, as if we knew what it means, as if it represented something fixed and unchanging rather than a living 'field' or force, like Life itself. The structure of the hexagram, with its open and yielding central lines, illustrates a truth about inner truth: that it draws on and puts its trust in emptiness and receptivity, allowing itself to be rediscovered every moment. Truth is life-giving, life-enhancing, and it starts as an inner movement, a shaping within the stillness of mind and body. But we must wait on it. When stillness extends into our depths, and we are without expectation or opinion, then we may find something true emerges. And it is likely to feel fresh and liberating, a new balance, not something old and rigid.

The hexagram presents the image of wind over water. When still water is touched by the wind – no matter how lightly – it springs to life as if animated. We cannot see the wind any more than we can see the animating force behind personal actions and choices; we apprehend its presence and its nature by its visible effects. Polonius's advice to Laertes (in *Hamlet*) quickens in us a recognition of truth: 'This above all: to thine own self be true, / And it must follow, as the night the day, / Thou canst not then be false to any man'. The reverse is also true: if we are false to ourselves, we cannot be true to others. But discerning what is 'true', within ourselves or within a situation, is not easy; we must be on the lookout for fleeting intuitions, glimpses of possibly unwelcome 'facts'. Like ripples on the still water of a quiet mind, these movements indicate the direction from which truth is coming.

The hexagram *Chung Fu* can also be taken to represent a meeting, perhaps the meeting of minds. If we face others with a closed mind, with our perception of the situation fixed and our decision a foregone conclusion, we have pre-empted the emergence of a fresh and relevant 'truth', one that might well lead us into a more creative engagement with each other, with the present situation, with life. If, as in the hexagram, we meet each other without prejudice, but with an open and curious mind and a willingness to really listen, we are ideally placed to learn. Where mistrust or self-interest prevents such a connection, we can, none the less, seek first to empty ourselves of fears or desires for a particular outcome, thus removing anything within our own mind or manner that might make the other person aggressive, suspicious, or defensive. Then we will be ready to turn our attention wholly towards the other, allowing them to speak as forcefully and earnestly as they might wish, without interruption or correction, at the same time truly listening and opening ourselves to their thoughts and their manner of thinking and feeling. Whatever the outcome, this honest effort to understand another person or point of view is valuable.

Inner truth does not reveal itself by magic or by simply wishing it to be so, nor is it something that is given or achieved for once and for all. The more profound the truth, the more empty and available must be the mind and heart of the individual seeker. This requires the development of a habit of attention and attentiveness to the Unseen – whether within or without – that will result in a quiet integrity and a strong and reliable intuitive capacity. An individual who has developed these qualities often affects others deeply, evoking in them a sort of echo or resonance.

The Changing Lines

9/1st If we want to penetrate to the very heart of a situation and effect real communication and change, we should not deceive ourselves by underestimating the path that lies before us. If we only deal with the situation superficially, or avoid personal commitment, no transformation will take place and nothing substantial will be achieved.

9/2nd The 'proof' of somebody being quietly grounded in inner truth is their willingness and ability to receive as well as to give, to be moved as well as to move. Everybody is touched and everybody benefits.

6/3rd Appearance and reality sometimes seem to be at odds. We may feel we are on the right track but do not seem to be able to get anywhere. At such a time we are not seeing clearly enough; we need to penetrate the surface 'noise' of the situation and find the quiet level beneath where truth dwells. Then we will recognize the way forward and not be deceived by false indications or hopes. No amount of agitation or insistence will achieve the required clarity.

6/4th Before a newly achieved sense of inner quiet and connection becomes established, it may be particularly vulnerable to challenge; but not everything that appears threatening is, in fact. Furthermore, in this atmosphere events or attitudes may become polarized, again, unnecessarily. Openness, curiosity, and trust will be conducive to stability, whereas mistrust or fear could undermine the progress that has already been made.

9/5th The foundations of inner truth and integrity are not achieved 'once-and-for-all'; on the contrary, sooner or later every gain must be relinquished in order for greater clarity and wisdom to be possible. Truth is a living energy, not a dead principle. We are called upon to simplify, release, and expand our experience periodically, to start the journey again. While this may involve some sacrifice, we will not lose anything that is of true worth.

9/top If we wait until the last moment to speak or act from inner truth, we are likely to overstate our views or feelings and run the risk of being misunderstood or even of provoking anger. It is probably best to learn from the situation that we have failed to address rather than try to jump in at the end. If we can truly connect with our innermost values now, we will be in a better position to speak up courageously in a future situation and may have learned some valuable lessons through exercising restraint.

62. Hsiao Kuo / Preponderance of the Small

Primary Trigrams

above *Chên* / The Arousing, Thunder
below *Kên* / Keeping Still, Mountain

Nuclear Trigrams

above *Tui* / The Joyous, Lake
below *Sun* / The Gentle, Wind, Wood

The name of this hexagram reflects its construction: yielding lines predominate, lying in the outer positions of the hexagram and, therefore, carrying the weight of responsibility for relating to the world. The image is of a bird, the two firm lines representing the body with the four yielding lines, the wings, supporting it. The times reflected by this hexagram are considered to be exceptional, when the lighter, outer element must bear the weight of a situation. Not surprisingly, conscientiousness and modesty are the most desirable qualities for such a time.

Another image associated with this hexagram is the pestle and mortar, with the top trigram representing the pestle and the lower the mortar. This image suggests a time of trial, of being 'ground down' to one's elements for some purpose that may well be unknowable at the moment. The pestle and mortar are generally associated with the chemistry laboratory, the artist's studio, or the kitchen, where materials are tested and transformed.

These attributes and associations to the hexagram have in common their transitory nature. A bird cannot fly too high or for too long without resting; a pestle and mortar prepares materials for another use, another process; a light and yielding individual cannot bear too much weight or responsibility indefinitely. So this is a time of transition. None the less, the times are such that, however small or powerless the individual in question may feel himself or herself to be, it is given to them to do what must be done at this moment. Given the constraints of this exceptional time, it would be unwise to embark on major changes or undertakings. Rather, we should simply attend to each moment to the best of our ability. Such a time can teach us a great deal; it requires awareness, gentle respect, patience, and trust. It is a time when small things matter a great deal and may have an effect much greater than their apparent size would suggest.

The Changing Lines

The overall balance of yielding, yin energies and firm, yang energies is disturbed at this time. As a result, both may be relatively ineffective, the yin degenerating into endless details – small things – and the yang unopposed or over-determined.

6/1st   If we respond to everything as soon as it appears on the scene, trying to capture and hold it, we risk not only exhaustion, but also ending up with very little to show for our efforts. On the other hand, if we can develop a degree of clarity and insight into the true worth of all that comes within our compass, we will establish a solid foundation for our choices. The growth of sound judgement requires patience, honesty, and self-knowledge.

6/2nd   While others may be chasing details, the well-grounded person deals with the task at hand. The development of flexibility and the achievement of long-term goals are both served in this way. The point of balance may change frequently, but if we remain attentive to it we will develop a capacity for discernment and equanimity.

9/3rd   Just when we think the situation cannot become any more uncertain is often the moment when it is further destabilized. Perhaps we have chosen to follow a somewhat reckless course of action in an attempt to resolve the uncertainty, to do something. Consulting with others whose judgement is trustworthy and proven is a good way to restrain impulsiveness. If we find ourselves resistant to this course of action, it is a good sign that we are in particular need of such grounding.

9/4th   Situations are particularly vulnerable to destabilization when containment is weak; then, one ill-considered action or the initiation of an unopposed new undertaking could have serious consequences. We need to develop a capacity for self-monitoring and self-restraint, and this arises most readily where there is a degree of natural reticence and modesty.

6/5th   Exceptional times require wise alliances. Issues of respect, trustworthiness, and shared, long-term goals need to be borne in mind. It is not a time for short-term, superficial, or blinkered interests to dominate, although there may well be pressure from just those quarters. Sound judgement and advice should be sought and valued highly, whether it is from within or without.

6/top   When we find ourselves 'out on a limb', apparently distanced from the arena of activity and experience with which we are familiar, we may wonder how we got into such a strange and uncomfortable position. Our inclination might be to re-establish a sense of safety, to get back 'home' as quickly as possible. But this could be a mistake. Life is brief; we are all just passing through, and such times can remind us of this and of the value, beauty, and precariousness of life. If, instead of being overwhelmed by difference, we risk opening ourselves to it and learn to respect the many forms that life takes, then we will have gained greatly from the experience.

63. Chi Chi / After Completion

Primary Trigrams

above *K'an* / The Abysmal, Water
below *Li* / The Clinging, Fire

Nuclear Trigrams

above *Li* / The Clinging, Fire
below *K'an* / The Abysmal, Water

The balance and order that we find in this hexagram – strong lines in strong positions, yielding lines in yielding – reflects not just a fleeting equilibrium but also, and more importantly, the completion of the journey through the book, the journey that started with difficulty (Hexagram 3, *Chun* / Difficulty at the Beginning), progressing through Youthful Folly (Hexagram 4, *Mêng*) and from thence to experiences of every sort of danger, conflict, family and social relationships, times of fullness and times of emptiness, and all the other conditions and situations represented by the hexagrams. The eye (*Li*) and the heart (*K'an*) are in balance, within and without (both primary and nuclear trigrams are *K'an* and *Li*); clarity of vision and depth of feeling are working hand in hand.

The name of this hexagram is 'After Completion', not simply 'Completion', and this points to a sensitive moment that scarcely exists in time; in fact, it is easy to miss it, like the pause between breaths. It is the instant when all elements slip into place and it has no sooner happened than time has moved on. For now, there is nothing more that can be done. The result may not be what we had hoped for or what we were aiming to achieve; none the less, it is time to own it, to consolidate it, if necessary, and to celebrate it in whatever way seems appropriate. The important thing is the acknowledgement that brings closure, and for that we must pause and become aware of this moment, surrender to it, celebrate it, and let it go.

The outer, or primary, trigrams in the present hexagram repre-sent order or balance in the present, however fleeting it may be; the inner, or nuclear, trigrams represent the tendency towards disorder and imbalance which is simply the natural, cyclical progression of life through time. The following hexagram reverses this structure. In both hexagrams these conditions of balance and imbalance complement and complete each other, both within and without. As *K'an* (Water) sinks to become groundwater, *Li* (Fire) rises to heaven. We may ask ourselves, what remains?

The Changing Lines

9/1st   The beginning of the end. A moment comes in any under-taking when we must recognize that we have achieved as much as we are likely to achieve and we must prepare ourselves to both honour the work that has been done and also accept what remains incomplete or imperfect in our eyes. Now is a moment to pause, to place the completion of this task in the wider context of the many tasks we may be called upon to address during life. We do our best and then we must let go, in the certain knowledge that another chal-lenge will soon present itself. If we fail to accept this we can wear ourselves out with resentment and grievance.

6/2nd   After completing a particular piece of work, whether inner or outer, we may feel at a loss, even bereft. Our inclination might be to cast around for something to fill the space now empty of purpose; we are generally uncomfortable with idleness and waiting. Yielding to such times means accept-ing them as they are and being willing to wait for as long as it takes for the next step to become evident. If we can even enjoy this period and make use of the time to review and reflect upon all that has happened or been achieved, then we will face the next challenge refreshed and wiser.

9/3rd   If we have played a clearly defined role in events and then find ourselves without such definition, we are very likely to feel both confused and frustrated. The establishment of clarity and order that has so recently been central to our experience disappears, leaving no signposts. It may be that others will shape future developments or that events apparently unconnected to us will gain significance and influence our lives. Whatever comes next is unclear, but we will be better prepared for it if we use the time to consolidate and make good the ground we have gained.

6/4th   No sooner is a temporary order established than it begins to evolve into the next period of disorder. The seeds of change lie within each moment and, if we resist or deny this truth and attempt to freeze time, it will only ensure that change, when it comes, is more violent and disruptive.

9/5th   Rarely are we alone in our achievements; others may have made our successes possible by their unobtrusive support without our even noticing them. It is hardly ever appropriate or helpful to boast or draw attention to oneself. When things fall into place we are, above all, being supported by the Tao, and that is not the personal property of anybody.

6/top   When a period of time that has been significant for us is drawing to a close, it is particularly important that we remain steadfast and calm and not try to relive or recapture the past, even if it was adventurous or fulfilling. When we are able to release what has gone before, no matter how good or bad it was at the time, we are able to live fully in the present, open to whatever form the future takes.

64. Wei Chi / Before Completion

Primary Trigrams

above *Li* / The Clinging, Fire
below *K'an* / The Abysmal, Water

Nuclear Trigrams

above *K'an* / The Abysmal, Water
below *Li* / The Clinging, Fire

The *I Ching* ends with a hexagram that signifies new beginnings or, rather, the eternal cycle of beginnings and endings. Formally, the work represented by this hexagram is that of transforming chaos into order, an order that is already implicit in the structure. If the previous hexagram points to the moments after completion and the need to pause and possibly effect closure, this hexagram addresses the moments before the next 'chapter' of life opens. Where *Chi Chi* concerns itself with a known action or process that has come to a close, *Wei Chi* stands before the Unknown and must yield to it, opening, emptying, and receiving before any action or choice can be initiated.

Whereas in the previous hexagram the lower primary trigram was *Li*, fire, and the upper was *K'an*, water, here they are reversed. The effect of fire on water is to create steam, if the two elements are handled properly; but with their positions reversed, their natures will tend in opposite directions, with fire flaming upwards and water sinking. If we wish to achieve something with such elements, we must understand their natures and work within that compass.

The outer, or primary, trigrams in the present hexagram represent imbalance in the present, however fleeting it may be; the inner, or nuclear, trigrams represent innate order or balance; that is, the natural, cyclical progression of life through time. The previous hexagram reverses this structure. Where the first two hexagrams in the *I Ching* present the dynamic energies of the Creative and the Receptive in their 'pure' state, these last two hexagrams emphasize the fleeting nature of their ever-changing balance and, in so doing, point to what lies between and beyond their dynamic interpenetration, moving us towards a mystery that transcends words.

The Changing Lines

6/1st   The period of time between an ending and a beginning can be stressful, and if we are feeling anxious we might be inclined to act impulsively, without reflection. There is a particular danger that these actions could be misperceived and could create divisions. The whole situation requires caution and patience and a preparedness to align oneself with the new set of conditions that are taking shape.

9/2nd   It can be particularly difficult to release the past when we have accomplished much and enjoyed recognition, but this may be exactly the time when others will come into prominence. The impulse to compete or achieve must sometimes be restrained and redirected towards the cultivation of awareness, receptivity, and insight. When the time comes for further decisions or actions, we are then less encumbered by an unhelpful drivenness.

6/3rd   The question we may face as we negotiate a transition into new and unknown territory is how to protect and nurture the most valuable aspects of what has gone before while embracing and responding to new challenges. In addition, some transitions move us into more profound areas of human experience and awareness than others, and the result may be both testing and transformative.

9/4th   Feelings of fear as well as excitement accompany all new beginnings, at any age. While we may wish to avoid appearing ignorant or clumsy or naïve, we cannot get anywhere unless we are prepared to seek advice, to risk showing our lack of experience and to push ahead, even if we do so awkwardly. Above all, what we need at such a time is a willingness to simply allow the energy of life to flow through our choices and actions. Perfectionism, envy, complacency, or self-pity can block the flow of life's energy.

Sometimes the most useful advice others can give us – or we can give ourselves – is, 'Just do it!'

6/5th   At times we hope to start a new chapter in life, but are not prepared to truly release what has gone before if it requires us to put an old conflict or misunderstanding behind us. It is remarkable with what determination we may cling to outworn prejudices or opinions, unaware that they are hindering our development. Such hardness sets us against the Tao and is, in effect, a rejection of life in all its beauty and complexity. It is not only a waste of energy, it is a waste of life itself.

9/top   The new situation is free to arise without hindrance, but we must always remember that the seeds of all things are in their beginnings. We should enter this time thoughtfully and gratefully; we have been given a new chance at life.

Appendix A

The Trigrams and the Sequence of Later Heaven

Familiarity with the trigrams grows as the *I Ching* is consulted and will be shaped by each individual's particular way of understanding the eight figures. The following comments are only signposts pointing to living energies and interrelationships that are beyond definition.

The trigrams represent the heavens, the seasons, the points of the compass, animals, man-made objects, spiritual principles, parts of the body, qualities of character, and much else besides. They do this by the association of the many – 'the ten thousand things', as the Buddhists would put it – with the few, the eight fundamental characters or trigrams. An exploration of the energies and attributes of the doubled foundation trigrams can be found in the Hexagrams section: numbers 1 and 2 (*Ch'ien* and *K'un*), 29 and 30 (*K'an* and *Li*), 51 and 52 (*Chên* and *Kên*), and 57 and 58 (*Sun* and *Tui*).

The eight trigrams look like this:

| Ch'ien | K'u | Chên | Sun | K'an | Li | Kên | Tui |

In Richard Wilhelm's translation of the *I Ching* (Wilhelm, 1989), two ways of ordering the trigrams are presented in the section entitled *Shuo Kua / Discussion of the Trigrams*; these are the Primal Arrangement (or Sequence of Earlier Heaven) and the Inner-World Arrangement (or Sequence of Later Heaven). In this section I will explore the latter arrangement, leaving the former to Appendix D.

> God comes forth in the sign of the Arousing; he brings all things to completion in the sign of the Gentle; he causes creatures to perceive one another in the sign of the Clinging; he causes them to serve one another in the sign of the Receptive. He gives them joy in the sign of the Joyous; he battles in the sign of the Creative; he toils in the sign of the Abysmal; he brings them to perfection in the sign of Keeping Still. [Wilhelm, 1989, p. 268]

This passage connects the trigrams sequentially in a narrative that rehearses and reminds us of the dramatic process of creation, whereby something altogether new appears and takes on form. 'God' can be thought of as representing the unconditioned, Life, the Tao, the One, without beginning or end. The thunderclap of *Chên*, The Arousing, located in the east, proclaims the moment of conception. Following this cataclysmic event, the new thing is shaped, given its form, completed through patience and perseverance, and this is represented by the trigram *Sun*, The Gentle. First, the seed, then the germination, the gestation, the passage of time necessary for a form to stabilize, to become itself and no other.

The trigram *Li*, located in the south, represents vision, the capacity to recognize other forms, to not confuse ourselves with other forms, to discern and distinguish difference. Fire is symbolized by *Li*, and the name of the trigram, The Clinging, reflects a sort of burning search for the truth of forms and formlessness. The yielding line in the centre of the trigram defines the quality of receptivity associated with *Li*, an emptiness that is fearless and unburdened by prejudice. The fire of creativity dies if it cannot breathe, if it is suffocated by falsity or the habitual.

In the sign of *Li* forms perceive one another, but they do not relate to one another; that is the realm of the Receptive, *K'un*, which represents the earth and devotion. The concept of service may seem out of place when we are considering creativity, yet we do not create in a vacuum; that which we create takes on a life of its own, to serve our purpose or that of others, for good or ill. We need the acute vision and honesty of *Li* to cut through our propensity for self-delusion. To 'earth' the energy of creativity by reflecting on what cause or end we might be serving is not only a wise, but also a creative act.

Aligning ourselves with the creative flow of life, of the Tao, can bring us moments of great joy, even in the midst of difficulties and conflict. Joy is a gift of Life, a sense of blessedness that arises spontaneously and unexpectedly. In the creative act, at the edge of becoming, a fierce joy may blaze up. The sign that represents this energy, this filling and uplifting of the heart and mind and spirit, is *Tui*. It enables us to continue.

'God' battles, in the sign of The Creative, *Ch'ien*, against the forces of inertia and entropy, against the age-old resistance to the new, the unknown. The act of creation is never easy, and, if we wish to live creatively, we must be prepared to fight for our vision, to champion it. The energy of The Creative is single-minded and determined; it needs to be, because it threatens the established order and, at one time or another, we are all identified with that order and derive our sense of safety from it. The ways in which we respond to the breakthrough of new movements, new challenges, new ideas – whether from without or within – will vary depending on the degree to which we are unsettled or threatened by them.

In the sign of The Abysmal, *K'an*, we must toil as 'God' toils, outlasting adversity, overcoming obstacles, keeping to our course, persevering in the face of doubt or despair, bearing sorrow and loss, surviving the abyss. This sign dwells in the north and represents winter.

In the final sign of the sequence, *Kên*, the creative act is perfected through stillness and the cessation of movement. Closure is achieved and with it, wholeness; transformation now becomes possible. The Mountain, which lies in the northeast, completes the cycle, and it is initiated again in the sign which lies next to it, *Chên*, The Arousing.

> Be completely empty.
> Be perfectly serene.
> The ten thousand things arise together;
> in their arising is their return.

Now they flower,
and flowering
sink homeward,
returning to the root.
The return to the root
is peace.
Peace: to accept what must be,
to know what endures.
In that knowledge is wisdom.

[Le Guin, 1997, p. 22]

Where ever I am going or
coming from
I am closer to the return

Appendix B

The Lines

First line. This place in the hexagram is yang in that it is an odd-numbered position. None the less, it is a position that is often linked with the counsel to proceed slowly, as it is outside the main action of the hexagram, or just at the beginning of it. In physical terms it is within the earth, and may even mean the feet of a person who is advancing. If a yin line occupies this position, there will naturally be reticence about proceeding hastily; in fact, that line might need encouragement to proceed in spite of the general advice for caution. If a yang line occupies it, the inclination might be to proceed too impulsively, or it might be that all the signs are favourable and so it should go ahead.

Second line. This line is in the middle of the lower primary trigram and is, in addition, the first line of the lower nuclear trigram, so the action has been joined. It is a yin or yielding place and, being central to the lower trigram, is seen to represent a moderate and modest attitude or person. This line is still linked with the earth, particularly the field, where the first appearance takes place. If it is occupied by a yang line, then, again, an unassuming attitude is ideal, strong but not motivated by a desire to advance too quickly or heap honours on oneself or seek visibility. If a yin line is here, the reticence is further emphasized and the line is considered to be 'correct' as well as 'central' and 'moderate'. ('Correct' because it is a yielding line in a yielding position; the same term is applied throughout the hexagram if the position and the line 'agree'.)

Third line. This is a firm or yang position, transitional between the lower and upper primary trigrams. It constitutes not only the top line of the lower primary trigram, but also the second line of the lower nuclear trigram and the bottom line of the upper nuclear trigram. It shares this characteristic of being part of three trigrams with the next line, and for that reason they are the lines that most reflect the action or process of the hexagram as a whole. As the two bottom lines represent earth, so the two middle lines represent humanity (and the two upper lines represent heaven or the enlightened person). In addition, the lines of the lower trigram are often described as 'coming', in other words, the action is developing towards a climax, whereas the lines of the upper trigram are described as 'going'; in other words, moving out of the sphere of action, having passed the climax. Because it lies at such an important juncture between 'coming' and 'going', this line reflects a time when discernment may be a particularly valuable quality.

Fourth line. A yielding position, sometimes considered to be one who serves. Depending on whether it is a 'correct' yin line that occupies this position or a strong yang line, the interpretation of behaviour will vary. In common with the third line, this line is in three trigrams, as the bottom line of the upper primary trigram, as the top line of the lower nuclear trigram, and as the middle line of the upper nuclear trigram. Although it plays an important part in the conditions and progress described by the hexagram, the hidden quality of this line means that its influence may not be readily obvious.

Fifth line. This line represents the 'Ruler'. It is a strong position and, lying in the upper reaches of the hexagram, it is associated with the enlightened individual, possibly a leader. The manner in which this line relates to – and is related to by – the other lines is important. It may not be the line that defines or encapsulates the essence of any particular hexagram or time, but it will always be influential, whether it is occupied by a yielding line or a firm one.

Sixth line. This is a yin, or yielding, position, isolated from the rest of the hexagram. The times that governed the counsel for the other positions are drawing to a close and do not really affect this line, nor are they affected by it, in general. At times this line represents the Sage who has moved through the demands and sufferings of life to a position of enlightened wisdom. In a general way, one can look at this line as representative of appropriate behaviour at the end of a particular set of conditions or challenges, and also as indicating the dangers and opportunities that might await the individual next, for as this line changes the whole hexagram moves into a new 'time'.

Appendix C

*Further Comments on the Process of Consulting the I Ching
and Instructions for Dividing the Yarrow Stalks*

One way of understanding the nature of the dialogue that can become possible with the *I Ching* is to see it as a sort of 'ink-blot' process. You look at a particular ink-blot and you see an old woman; I look at the same one, and I see a herd of deer running across the page. Another person clearly sees a dog and cat fighting. The same can happen with clouds, or 'faces' seen in rock formations. We look and what we see is a combination of what is 'out there' and what is 'in here'. When we read the commentary on a particular hexagram the effect will be different in the case of each individual, because each of us will relate it to our own lives, so the hexagram becomes a sort of vessel or screen into which, or on to which we project our own dilemmas or hopes or fears. The *I Ching* offers not just a mirror image of ourselves but, rather, a reflection of our situation that, like abstract art, moves around us and shows us dimensions and facets that we cannot see; it suggests how we might have got to where we are, where we might go if we carry on as we are. Our situation will be similar in its general energies and issues to situations that have occurred throughout the ages and always will occur, as they are the natural expression of the vitality of the forces operating in nature and in human nature. When we consult the *I Ching*, we bring the personal details and questions of our own life to this transpersonal template; we add the flesh of this moment in time to the skeleton of similar moments throughout time.

Is it essential to throw the coins (or manipulate the yarrow stalks) or could we just open to a page 'at random' and read it? I believe the most important aspect of the whole process of consulting the *I Ching* rests in the care and thoughtfulness with which the individual prepares herself. It takes time and commitment to sit quietly, to gather oneself and one's thoughts, to review the situation in which one finds oneself and what effect it seems to be having, to reflect on the nature of the particular worry or question that one would like to bring to the *I Ching*. Throwing the coins after doing this reflecting simply offers the best possible chance of bringing as much of oneself as possible into the present, this moment – Me, Here, Now. While the *I Ching* can certainly be used simply in this 'ink-blot' way, personally, I believe that a more lively and complex interaction is taking place. Jung used the term 'synchronicity' to denote the process by which apparently unconnected events are linked 'acausally', which is simply a way of saying that we cannot determine or establish the cause. We have all experienced and wondered at 'coincidences', events that come together in an apparently meaningful way (although the word is also applied when there seems to be no significance). Most of us are able to accept and embrace the strangeness of these events, some of us find meaning and guidance in them, others argue against and dismiss their very existence. The important point is that what is meaningful is always going to be personal: the connection between events and the meaning of that connection is first made or experienced within, and, to that extent, is incontestable. The notion of proof or disproof is irrelevant, because, in Jung's words, we are dealing with a 'psychic fact'. When I sit down to consult the *I Ching* I am choosing to place myself at the centre of this moment. I still my mind and body and listen from a place of intense and open concentration. For me, it does not make sense to imagine that the consequences of this activity are unrelated to the state of mind and body that I have chosen, purposefully, to establish. In terms of Pascal's wager about the existence of God, it is probably a better bet to assume that there are complex and meaningful connections between events than to opt for a world devoid of the amazing and the irreducible.

For this reason, using yarrow stalks rather than coins might be considered to be preferable. Constructing a hexagram takes far longer when yarrow stalks are used, probably between ten and fifteen minutes, whereas the coins can be thrown six times in less than a minute. The entire ritual of the yarrow stalks – dividing, counting, combining, subtracting, placing correctly – requires patience and attention. Shortcuts might suggest themselves, but the orderly completion of the ritual supports the intention to establish a quiet and focused mind and is also satisfying in itself. Of course, using the coins also requires focus and care, and the ease with which a hexagram can be constructed is greatly in its favour, but it does not require the same degree of patience and sustained attention. A further advantage to using the yarrow stalks lies in the greater degree of uncertainty, or rather, the element of 'spin' that accompanies the first division for each line. Whereas with the coins the chances are always 50–50 for heads or tails, for complex mathematical reasons, in the first division of the stalks the chances are 3–1 in favour of an unbroken line. The imbalance or 'oddness' of this element seems to me to replicate an oddness that permeates life, a lopsidedness that precludes prediction and frustrates all efforts to achieve stasis, to 'fix' things, for once and for all.

The first move is a subtraction: one stalk is set aside. The remaining forty-nine are divided at random and placed side by side. From the right-hand bundle one stalk is removed and placed between the third and fourth fingers of the left hand. Then the bundle on the left is picked up and counted off in multiples of four. When four or fewer stalks remain, they are placed between the second and third fingers of the left hand. Then the bundle on the right is picked up and is also counted off in multiples of four, the remaining stalks being placed between the first and second fingers of the left hand. (Placing the stalks in this way ensures that the counting is done accurately and can be checked at any moment. It also leaves the hands relatively free to do the counting off.) The number of stalks in the left hand will be nine or five. For this first division only, one is subtracted from the total, giving eight or four. Four is considered to be a whole unit, firm, light, yang, and is, therefore, assigned the value three. Eight is twice four and is assigned the value two. This completes the first division and is the same as tossing one coin. A note should be made of the value obtained and to this will be added the next two results. To continue the construction of the first line of the hexagram, the stalks already counted and held in the left hand are placed to one side. The remaining stalks are gathered up and divided again in the same way as before. This time the result will be eight or four and the same method is employed to assign a value of two or three. When this has been done, the stalks in the left hand are again set aside and the remaining stalks gathered up and divided for a third time. The three values obtained will be the equivalent of throwing three coins once and their total will be six, seven, eight or nine. Even numbers (six and eight) are considered to be yielding, or yin, and are indicated by a broken line. Odd numbers (seven and nine) are considered to be firm, or yang, and are indicated by a solid or unbroken line. This first line will be at the bottom of the hexagram and should be noted with both its numerical value and the corresponding sign, allowing space above it for the remaining five lines. If a six or a nine is obtained, this line will be seen to be changing and will be treated differently from a seven or eight. (See Introduction.) The fifty stalks are now all gathered up again and the same procedure is employed to obtain the remaining five lines, starting with the subtraction of one stalk. In all, the stalks will be divided eighteen times.

The procedure for constructing a hexagram using the coins is described in the Introduction.

Appendix D

The Sequence of Earlier Heaven and the Tao

In Appendix A, the arrangement of the trigrams known as the Sequence of Later Heaven, or the Inner-World Arrangement, was explored. In this section, the Sequence of Earlier Heaven, or the Primal World Arrangement, will be examined. In the former, movement can be visualized as occurring around the circumference of a circle in a clockwise direction. This sequence records the act of creation from the explosive moment of birth, through the taking on of a form, thence to the perception of and relationship with other forms in space, to the individual experience of joy, the challenge of creativity, the sorrows that accompany a profound connection to life, and finally, the perfection of acceptance. As a rough blueprint of the complex journey from birth to death of a universe or an individual or an idea, it is both recognizably congruent with our experience while also offering us food for thought.

On the more or less microscopic level of our brief lives it is easy to believe that cause and effect operate in a direct and uncomplicated – linear – manner. Life is not so haphazard that we are unable to make choices, to plan and carry out projects. However, from experience we also recognize that it is not as simple as that. The Sequence of Earlier Heaven portrays the forces at work in the cosmos – still symbolized by the eight trigrams – as constantly interacting and interpenetrating each other, contracting and expanding, enfolding and unfolding, constructing and constituting an infinite web of influences. Everything is present at all times and the movement, if we can call it that, is not about a sequential process of creation, as in the Sequence of Later Heaven, but rather about another process whereby events – actions and consequences, macrocosmic and microcosmic – are enfolded back into the matrix to be reshuffled into the shifting 'genetic code' of future events. Nothing is lost or inconsequential.

The characteristic fields of potential represented by each of the eight trigrams and their associated attributes shape energetic connections as would a magnet. We might (imperfectly) visualize the infinite number of connections thus formed as a net. If we imagine this net as lying invisibly beneath the surface appearances and phenomena of life, then when we consult the *I Ching* we are effectively reaching down and drawing the net to the surface. As all points on the net are dynamically connected, whether or not we can see those connections, we will always be drawing up or affecting every other point. Moreover, in consciously making the choice to draw up the net, we introduce a sort of charge or a new intricacy to it; we add our particular energy or flow at that moment to that point of contact. We choose to become what we are anyway, by virtue of our aliveness: co-creators and participants in the unfolding of Life, in the movement of the Tao.

This book would be incomplete if I did not attempt to articulate my personal understanding of Tao. My version of the *I Ching* springs from, and is informed by, experiences and intuitions concerning the responsiveness of that which is apparently 'external' to that which is deemed to be 'internal', and vice versa. The image of a net that I invoked above only partially reflects the totality of this relationship; to add flow – movement and direction – to the image places it in space–time and hints at the medium in which the net lies. Tao is the net, the flow, the medium, the direction; it is the response and the relationship; it is space–time. We do not need to have a sophisticated understanding of Taoism to become sensitive to our own flow, and thus to our relationship with the greater flow.

By monitoring the extent to which we feel aligned or misaligned with our lives at any given moment, we can grow to appreciate the distinction between when we are 'in' our Tao, our flow, and when we are not. Tao is the Way, and the way things work, but, to conclude with the words with which I chose to begin this book, the Tao that can be named is not the true Tao.

Appendix E: The Grid

above → below ↓	Ch'ien	Chên	K'an	Kên	K'un	Sun	Li	Tui
Ch'ien	1	34	5	26	11	9	14	43
Chên	25	51	3	27	24	42	21	17
K'an	6	40	29	4	7	59	64	47
Kên	33	62	39	52	15	53	56	31
K'un	12	16	8	23	2	20	35	45
Sun	44	32	48	18	46	57	50	28
Li	13	55	63	22	36	37	30	49
Tui	10	54	60	41	19	61	38	58

References

Barks, C., & Moyne, J, (Trans.) (1995). *The Essential Rumi*. San Francisco, CA: Harper.

Browning, R. (1956). *Poetry and Prose*. London: Oxford University Press.

Eliot, T. S. (1963). *Collected Poems 1909–1962*. London: Faber and Faber.

Geddes, G. (1995). *Looking for the Golden Needle: An Allegorical Journey*. Plymouth: MannaMedia.

Heider, J. (1985). *The Tao of Leadership*. Aldershot: Wildwood House.

LeGuin, U. K. (1997). *Lao Tzu, Tao Te Ching: A Book About The Way and the Power of The Way*. Boston, MA: Shambhala.

Nomura, Y. (1983). *Desert Wisdom: Sayings from the Desert Fathers*. London: Eyre & Spottiswoode.

Wilhelm, R. (1989). *I Ching or Book of Changes*. London: Arkana (Penguin).